The Feldman Method:

The Words and Working Philosophy
of the World's
Greatest Insurance Salesman

Andrew H. Thomson

All rights reserved. No part of this publication may be
reproduced, stored in a retrieval system, or transmitted in any form or
by any means, electronic, mechanical, photocopying or otherwise,
without the prior permission of the copyright owner.

© Copyright 1969 by Andrew H. Thomson
Published by BN Publishing

Cover Design: Talia Kauff

www.bnpublishing.com

info@bnpublishing.com

For information regarding special discounts for bulk purchases, please contact
BN Publishing at

sales@bnpublishing.net

Foreword

Ben Feldman is one of the nation's dozen top salesmen. In his own field, life insurance sales, he stands alone. I feel no misgivings about describing him with the much over-used word, "genius."

But Ben Feldman doesn't regard himself as one. He feels that his success is the result of a keen desire to rise above his less-than-affluent boyhood, and a gift for intelligent hard work and long hours.

Success, though, seldom comes from incentive and grueling work alone. They must be present, but there must also be a special approach, a different way of doing things.

Ben Feldman has developed a sales method peculiarly his own. In this volume, I have attempted to describe it in a detailed organized fashion for the first time.

The story of Ben's Method and Ben's life (they're inseparable) is told here, wherever possible, in Ben's own words assembled from talks, interviews, seminars, sales meetings, articles about Ben and articles by Ben. I've also used tapes of real and simulated interviews. I've talked with Ben's policy owners, his friends and business associates, and with his wife and children.

But the most important source of my material is Ben himself. I've known him since 1941—the year before he began his now famous career with New York Life.

Foreword

The perceptive reader will note occasionally that, with no attempt at subtlety, I have let Ben Feldman pay tribute to my influence on his success. Perhaps this furnishes a revealing glimpse of both author and subject. My pride in my long association and great friendship with the most remarkable man I've ever known, is, in a sense, a measure of my own self-esteem. And Ben's open acknowledgement of the role I have played in his success story, while wholly exaggerated, is entirely characteristic.

If it were I who were to single out the person most responsible for Ben's success, I would have to select his wife, Fritzie. The greatest "sale" Ben Feldman ever made was when he persuaded that young schoolteacher from Beaver Falls to become his wife. She's been his inspiration, his sounding board, his support when things went wrong, his severest critic. If Ben Feldman is a great man, it may be because there's a great woman behind him.

Andrew H. Thomson

August, 1969

CONTENTS

Foreword v

PART I
MEET BEN FELDMAN

1. Becoming a Millionaire Through Selling 3

PART II
MAKING THE SALE

2. Planning (I) 11
3. Planning (II) 19
4. Preparation 27
5. Prospecting 35
6. The Call 43
7. The Interview
   I: Attitude 55
8. The Interview
   II: Presentation 63

PART III
SOLVING THE PROBLEMS

9. The Problem of the Shrinking Estate 77
10. The Problem of the Close Corporation 85

Contents

11. The Problem of the Keyman 95
12. The Problem of Keeping a Business Going 103
13. The Problem of Insuring the Uninsurables 111
14. The Problem of Paying the Premiums 117
15. The Problem of the Young Man 125
16. Tailored Dollars 133

PART IV

FELDMANISMS: BEN'S POWER PHRASES AND CAPSULE COMMENTS

17. 'Secrets' of Success 143
18. Power Phrases and Sales-Talk Ideas 159
19. Disturbing Questions 183
20. Tools for Making Sales 189
21. Answering Objections 197

PART V

THE SUCCESS FORMULA: MAKING THE METHOD WORK

22. Obstacles to Success and How to Overcome Them ... 207
23. Guidelines to Success and How to Apply Them 217

Part I
Meet Ben Feldman

BECOMING A MILLIONAIRE THROUGH SELLING | 1

'Only a fool learns by his own experiences'

He's in his mid-fifties, short and heavyset. His tightly curled hair is almost all grey now and still in slow retreat. His voice is soft with just the hint of a lisp. He is gentle and humble. If you passed him on the street, you'd never guess he's one of the world's greatest salesmen. He's Ben Feldman.

In a single sale, he has registered $10,000,000.

In a single year—$56,000,000.

In a single career with one company since 1942, Ben Feldman has written individual life-insurance coverages totalling more than $300,000,000.

Meet Ben Feldman

In a professionally oriented business, where a $1,000,000-a-year production can win coveted membership in the elite *Million Dollar Round Table,* Ben Feldman's nearly $10,000,000-a-year average over a quarter century sets him magnificently apart.

No one in the history of life-insurance salesmanship comes close to him.

Alone, he has put more life insurance on the books than have some 1,000 of about 1,500 life insurance companies in America!

And he did it all working out of a little town on the Ohio River: East Liverpool, with a population of 22,000—about the same figure it boasted 20 years ago!

Ben Feldman transforms the impossible into the commonplace:

In 1955, no one ever seriously thought a life insurance salesman could top $10,000,000 in annual sales.

In 1956, Feldman topped it.

In 1959, $20,000,000 a year in production was a wild dream, so fantastic that no one in the business had ever even thought about it.

Except Ben!

In 1960, he turned that dream into a reality.

By 1966, Feldman had already become the first man to pass the unreachable $25,000,000-a-year goal, but not even his most passionate admirers—and he has become a legend in his own lifetime—could possibly conceive of his making another major gain.

BECOMING A MILLIONAIRE THROUGH SELLING

In 1966, Feldman cracked the $50,000,000 barrier.

In 1967, he did it again!

And he's still raising his sights—even more important, he's raising the sights of the life insurance business along with him.

The $1,000,000 policy that once strained the life underwriter's credibility now scarcely lifts his eyebrow.

Feldman showed that substantial seven figure sales could be made ... even repeat sales!

Now, the entire industry is making them.

Ben Feldman has become the pace-setter of life insurance selling. Because of Ben, hundreds of salesmen have been running faster to bigger goals. The lives of thousands have been enriched because, with his heart, Feldman believes there's nothing the human mind and spirit can't achieve. In life insurance, this attitude has virtually obliterated the concept of the impossible.

Only one impossibility would seem to remain.

The impossibility of beating Ben Feldman—and, of course, it's conceivable that the man who will "achieve the impossible" is reading this book. But it won't be easy.

For Ben, the toughest instrument in the orchestra to play is second fiddle. He must be No. 1, and he must *stay* No. 1. In 1965, for example, his new sales reached $20,000,000 exhausting his prospect list. In the first two months of 1966, several other New York Life agents surged ahead of him in sales. Any other man might have ignored them while he rested on last year's laurels. But not Ben. He struck vigorously, and by April he had $8,000,000 in sales on 30 different lives. He was ahead of the pack again—and he has never been passed in annual sales since!

Meet Ben Feldman

He has led his company's sales force for 15 consecutive years.

His unyielding competitive spirit kept him there. In 1968, one of New York Life's top-flight agents placed a *jumbo*—a $5,000,000 policy. He jumped ahead of Ben with only five months to go with an almost unbeatable lead in first-year commissions—the yardstick by which his company's agents are ranked. With only one month left in the year, Ben had not only closed the gap but his total first-year commissions surpassed his friendly rival by a margin equal to the total commissions of the next four agents in this group.

Ben enjoys competition. He likes to run. "I find it much harder not to run, than to run," he says. Beneath his unassuming manner is a passionate desire to succeed and exceed, backed up by an apparently inexhaustible supply of mental and physical energy. His running has given him an annual income well up into six figures and has, of course, made him a millionaire.

And it's done something else. Something that Ben regards as far more important. These 3,000 people who are the real beneficiaries of his energy and talent—the people of Eastern Ohio over whom he's thrown a more-than $300,000,000 mantle of protection—these people believe in Ben. Said a well-to-do East Liverpool dairy farmer who has done business with Ben for 20 years: "I have never known a nicer, squarer or better man."

What's the success formula of this modest man who was forced to drop out of high school classes in his freshman year? Who started life and failed as a $10-a-week egg salesman? Who was once rejected for a sales job because he couldn't pass the aptitude tests? What are the paths of action that this friendly, soft-spoken man takes that enables him to upgrade one policy-owner from $2,000 to $16,000,000? What makes the life insurance world take for granted that the sales records he sets today will be broken by him tomorrow? What does Ben Feldman do that sets him apart? What are his secrets of success?

"But there aren't any secrets!" proclaims Ben.

What he really means is that he has made his "secrets" available to all. Over the years, he has taken many hours from his seven-day week to tell about his techniques and interviews to insurance people from New York to Australia.

Why does he do it? Why should a man with such fierce, competitive spirit divulge so freely and unselfishly the sales techniques and power phrases to which he attributes his success?

There is no one simple explanation because Ben Feldman is a man of great complexity. Perhaps like most great salesmen—indeed great men in all walks of life—Ben is also part evangelist and missionary. He measures his success not by his own material accomplishments alone, but by his impact on others—his influence for good not just on his salesman peers, but also on the people they serve.

The "Feldman Method" (which, he admits, he learned from the experiences of others) is essentially procedural. It is a step-by-step, well-planned, logically thought-out pattern for action leading to a sale. Plus an unconquerable desire to win.

In this volume, the Feldman Method is presented for the first time in a detailed, organized fashion. Told, for the most part, in Ben's own words, it is designed as a handbook for success for all salesmen, not just those in life insurance, a guide on how to think big, and make sales that count . . . sale after sale after sale.

Here, then, is the track that Ben Feldman runs on. And here's how he runs on it.

Meet Ben Feldman

"Only a fool," says Ben, "learns from his own experiences. The wise man learns from the experiences of others."

Learn from the experience of this great salesman. His track could be yours!

Part II

Making the Sale

*"Find the problem and the solution—
and you'll make the sale."*

PLANNING (I) | 2

'Goals are everything'

"You must have a plan!" Ben counsels.

And the plan begins when you set your goals. Production goals. Earning goals. Satisfaction goals! "These are what make you run. These are the prizes at the end of the race. This is what you'll get out of life. Goals to me are everything!"

He recalls his first major goal. It was $35 a week. "And to me," notes Ben, "that was fabulous."

The year was 1938. The place was Salineville, Ohio, and he was earning $10 a week selling butter and eggs for his father. Ben was 26 years old (birthdate September 7, 1912). He had

Making the Sale

met "the loveliest girl in the world," Freda Zaremberg, a schoolteacher, "and after a while, one day I proposed marriage. I'll never forget what she said:

" 'Do you intend to support me on $10 a week?'

"Then I knew I had to do something. But where do you look for a job in a little town like this?

"It just so happened that a friend of mine was with a small industrial life insurance company on what was called a debit. And he was earning $35 a week, but to me that was fabulous. He indicated there might be an opening. And so I went down and applied for the job."

When Feldman tells this story, he often shows a picture of himself as he looked at 26. "The picture will tell you," he says laughingly, "why I didn't get the job. A hayseed, a hick from the sticks—how could I sell life insurance? They told me I didn't look the part. I didn't measure up. Everything was wrong. A husky farm kid that went down the street dressed in overalls! 'You don't look like anybody who should go pounding on a door talking about life insurance,' And maybe they were right. But you know ...

"When you tell me I can't do something, you may be right, *but I don't believe it*. Nothing builds a fire under me more than if I'm told I *can't* do something. Maybe I can't—but I'm sure going to try."

Ben always had extraordinary self-assurance. "While I didn't know anything about life insurance, I knew this: if *you* can do it—*I* can do it. If *you* can make $35 a week—*I* can make $35 a week. I always felt I could do anything the next man can." His refusal to take no for an answer ("Well, you know, I don't hear a man when he says, 'no.' ") finally impressed that small

Planning (I)

company manager. He decided to let Feldman try. "I got the job. They gave me a debit and a collection book, and they told me to go to work."

"We didn't know if he was going to earn anything," his wife (every one calls her Fritzie) recollects. From butter and eggs to 25 cents-a-week industrial policies was an enormous leap. "Everyone was worried when Ben started to sell life insurance. But Ben said to me: 'If I decide to dig ditches, I'll dig the best ditches. And if I'm going to sell life insurance, I'll be the best life insurance salesman there is.'"

That $35-a-week goal wasn't easy to achieve, but Ben did it. Then he moved his sights up a bit. $45. $60. Despite the fact they broke up his debit, and shared it with other agents, his earnings still increased. He set his goals higher. In less than three years, he was a top agent in the company, averaging almost $105 a week. It was late in 1941 and most salesmen his age would have been wholly content. But not Ben.

"Any man who is perfectly satisfied with the way he is living, or the way he is doing his job, is in a rut. If he has no driving urge to be a better person, or do a better job, then he is standing still. And, as any business man will tell you, standing still is the same as going backwards. One of the greatest virtues a man can have is a total inability to be completely satisfied with his own work."

Ben was restive. He knew of other life insurance salesmen —"ordinary" agents who were "getting out and making more money, making progress." But he was standing still. He didn't have much time to sell—*really* sell. Sure, he was making two to three little sales a day, but collections kept biting more deeply into his limited selling time.

"On a debit, primarily you're a collector. First, you collect. Then, if you have any time left, you sell. And I didn't like to collect. I just didn't! I compared my income with what full-time *salesmen* were making. The contrast was incredible. And I felt—my friend, if *you* can do it, *I* can do it."

So he set a new kind of goal for himself—full-time selling. But it was a goal he knew he could never reach in his debit company. He'd have to find another life insurance company where he didn't have to spend time collecting. That company was to be New York Life.

"So I went to see them and they weren't sure I'd fit into their operations at all." But Ben had set himself a goal and he was determined to reach it. He was deaf to New York Life's reservations and kept coming back with reasons why he would make good. At one juncture he said: "You toss me out this door, and I'll come back in that one." He was selling *himself*, and finally they "bought" him.

"They weren't really sure I could make it and I knew it was going to be tough. Nowadays, the agent has a built-in cushion: he's entitled to a guarantee—to some money regularly —come what may. But in 1942—no sales, no money. Either you sold or you didn't eat. The debit company was sure I *wouldn't* eat. 'You can come back to us at the end of 90 days,' they said. Their vice president told me: 'This ordinary business isn't for you. You'll fall flat on your face!' "

"Well, maybe I would fall on my face—but, you know, I had to find out for myself. I had to make the change. A man has to let go of lower things and reach for the higher!"

In his first year with New York Life (he joined the company February 15, 1942; he was 29 years old, and his first son,

Richard, had just been born), he was still thinking debit-size policies—thinking small.

"If you think small, your cases will be small. I was writing a lot of cases, very small cases, a lot of $500 policies, not very much volume." By the end of the year, he had delivered 168 policies (his lifetime average is 172)—but his volume was only $252,128.

By mid-1944, Feldman's new goals had been met—he'd paid for more than $500,000 in the past 12 months. But he was still dissatisfied. Sure his volume was up, and his average policy had grown to nearly $2,000 from his rookie-year's $1,300 but it wasn't enough. To make matters worse, the key to Ben's escalating goals was better prospects, and he believed he was running out of prospects. He needed help—but even more important, he was in trouble and he'd listen.

But let Ben tell it the way he told the Editor of New York Life's field magazine a year later.

"After carefully listening to all my troubles, Andy Thomson, my Manager, said: 'Ben, how would you like to do something no one from our company has done in Ohio in many a year?'

" 'What?' I answered, a bit curiously—and, I might add, cautiously.

" '*Make the Million Dollar Round Table in the next 12 months.*'

"If I hadn't been sitting at the time, I would have fallen down. I thought to myself, 'Andy's gone crazy!' Here I've driven 40 miles to tell him I've written myself out of prospects—and I don't know where my next application is coming from—and he asks me if I'd like to 'make the Million Dollar Round Table!' What could I lose? So, I said, 'Sure—but how?'

"And Andy told me how I could do it: 'Become an expert in program selling. Get into the small business insurance field. There's a tremendous potential in small business cases but you'll have to do some studying. You are going to have to go after the better and the bigger cases—and remember: *You can't kill an elephant with a pop-gun!*'

"When he told me this," Feldman admits, "I knew what had been wrong. I hadn't been thinking big enough. I just didn't have a big enough goal."

Now he had the goal. And he went after it relentlessly with that tremendous supply of sheer physical energy that still never lets his mind make appointments his body can't keep. His volume trebled and, by June 1945, he had earned his first membership in the Million Dollar Round Table with 224 sales for just over $1,100,000. And he had been in ordinary sales only a little over three years!

He had learned how to *think big*. "The size of your cases will be governed by your thinking. Think big and your cases will be big. Most men exchange their lifetimes for much too little. Don't be afraid to think big. Raise your own sights, then you can raise your prospect's sights. *Think* big and you'll *be* big."

Think big. And then think bigger: "Your goals have to be big enough to get you excited. That makes you run. But once you've reached them," Ben explains, "they don't excite you any longer. Whatever I did yesterday, today no longer looks big. It looks small. I can't get excited about anything that looks small. Only something big.

Planning (I)

"Old goals don't excite. You have to set a goal, and, regardless of what it is, once it's attained, replace it. With a new goal—a bigger goal. Don't be afraid if it gets bigger and bigger. You know the difference between $100,000 and $1,000,000? Only one zero! If you're not afraid to think bigger, it's amazing how much bigger you can become. Dream! Don't be afraid to dream. Three hundred thousand looked big 30 years ago. Now, seventy million wouldn't frighten me. Set a big goal. Nothing builds a bigger fire under me than a *bigger* goal. Then a bigger...."

It's Ben's unremitting drive toward these new goals that has broken sales record after sales record. And will break new sales records tomorrow.

"There's always some new goal way up ahead. There's always something I can look up to. There's always something bigger."

PLANNING (II) | 3

'A track to run on'

But if a goal is something to run *to*, Ben must have something to run *on*. A path of action that will carry him directly to his goal in the shortest time. A track. *A track to run on.* Here is how he told it to 2,000 fellow Million Dollar Round Table members in June 1966.

"Andy Thomson gave me my first track to run on. Do you know what it was? Andy put it all in eight words. 'Three cases a week and keep it simple.' That's all. *Simple.* That's the track he put me on when I came to New York Life in 1942. That's the track I'm still running on today. I was writing three cases a week *then*. I'm not doing anything differently *now*. I'm writing three cases a week now—and I still keep it simple! The only thing that has changed is my average size policy."

Ben knew the importance of the deadline. Three cases *a week. Each* week. *Every* week. 52 weeks a year. *Meet that deadline.*

"Goals aren't enough! You need goals plus deadlines. Goals big enough to get excited about, and a deadline to make you run. One isn't much good without the other, but together they can be tremendous."

But that deadline, he emphasizes, must be realistic. If you can't meet it, it only means frustration and failure. Three cases in seven days is a deadline Ben can easily meet. "It's a simple track. It had to be or I couldn't have stayed on it." It's a track, moreover, that leads right to the multi-million dollar goals and he explains how:

"You know, if I said to you, you've got to do $3,000,000 this year—*you must* do it this year, no ifs, ands, or buts—you'd be frightened, wouldn't you? That frightens you. You can't do it. Too big. So let's break that apart into little pieces. Let's break that $3,000,000 down by timing. First into months. That's $250,000. Still too big? Let's break it down. Into weeks. Let's take that $250,000 and divide by four. Now you don't have to write $250,000. You only have to write about $60,000.

"Still too big? Yes. How many people want $60,000? How many people are even willing to listen to you? Where are you going to write $60,000 this afternoon? It still frightens you. So let's continue to break it down. It's still too big, so you're going to break it down by three. Three cases a week. Now divide three into $60,000. Now you're down to something you're not afraid of. You've done that lots of times! Three cases a week.

Planning (II)

You've got a track to run on. Now it can be done. Make your goal big enough to be exciting. Then break it down into little pieces so it's *do-able*."

But the track that Ben runs on is not only made up of deadlines. What's the action itself?

"It's merchandising simple packages. You break your case down into *ideas*—very simple packages. *Very* simple packages. Each is designed to say, *Discount Your Tax*, or *Buy Your Partner's Interest*, or *Insure One Year's Profits*, or *Guarantee a Market for Your Company* . . ." What each package does is to clearly and dramatically "point out each prospect's *need* for life insurance in such a way that—*he has to do something about it*."

This, then, is the *basic track* Ben Feldman runs on.

It's the big quota broken down into *timing*, then into packaged *ideas*, and, most important, into *three applications a week*. "If I write those three applications *every* week," he asserts with confidence, "then I know I'm moving along."

* * * * * *

But it's a race to meet these deadlines *every* week, and Ben couldn't win if he didn't make every minute count. He works hard, of course. Long hours. His work day begins before 8. It ends 12—even 16—hours later. Then he studies for another two hours. That goes on six days a week. And Sunday? He'll often work until 3 o'clock in the afternoon after giving himself the special treat of not starting until 10 a.m.

He's been doing this since 1942 with infrequent short vacations. (He loves to fish, even though he gets seasick!)

"But there's no easy way. You kid yourself if you're looking for an easy way. There's no such animal. There's nothing for nothing! I don't think there's any easy formula for writing one case a week or ten cases a week; or one million a year, or five million a year, or ten million a year. You delude yourself, if you think so. You've got to spend time if you want to get your job done properly."

Time—lots of it—that's the price he pays for overwhelming success. But there isn't enough time. Even his 12-hour day, six or seven days a week ("It's that—and more.") is too short.

To meet his deadlines, he has to make each 24 hours the equivalent of 48 hours, or longer. He must make each minute count for two. Or three. Or more. He does it!

Through *scheduling*.

"Successful work stems from organization, from scheduling your time and your efforts. It takes time to think out a schedule. But that's a small price to pay compared with the price you must pay without an organized work schedule. You have just so much time. How would you like to spend it? *Time? Use it or lose it! Take your choice!* You use it best when you organize your time so you'll put in a full day's work."

Ben usually organizes his next week's activities in the uninterrupted seclusion of his office on Sunday. He nails down each day's schedule the night before. "I know tonight where I'm going tomorrow, because if I wait until tomorrow it's too late. I wouldn't know where I'm going or what I'm going to do."

He uses a tool to help him organize. It's his company's *Plan and Work Book*. "It tends to crystallize where you'd like to go, whom you'd like to see, why you'd like to see them, *what*

Planning (II)

you want to talk about. I've used this ever since my first year, and I'm still using it. Time. It's the biggest asset any man has. I don't want to lose it. I want to use it to do the things I do best."

And the thing he does best is selling. But by his third year with New York Life, with his volume swelling through many applications and dozens of interviews to prepare for each week, he found himself being gradually caught in the paperwork trap; the more business he did, the less time he had to go out and sell. "Andy Thomson came to my rescue again. He always had the answer—he told me to hire a secretary.

"I wasn't too happy about it," Ben admits. "To me, that meant spending more money. And I was a little concerned . . . would I have enough work to keep her busy? But Andy convinced me, even if I had to borrow the money. It was the *right* thing to do. That's how you *grow!* So I hired a girl.

"And Andy was *right.* She did give me time to keep doing what I was best qualified to do . . . instead of spending my time on something that, frankly, *she* was better qualified to do. In the year after I hired her, my sales production *doubled.* And we've been moving ever since."

Ben had discovered another major "secret" of success. He had learned that he could buy time. By hiring employees, by giving them good office equipment to work with, he could free himself of the thousands of details that go with a sale. "I don't like details. I just like to go out and talk with someone who has a very real problem when I think I've got the answer."

To those who hesitate about taking on additional help because of the cost, Ben suggests this test: "Do it or don't do it. What's the price? If you *don't* do it, you'll be doing the work a $2.00-an-hour girl can do and so your time will be worth only

$2.00 per hour. But if you hire someone, you'll be free to do those things you do best—with no limit on your earnings."

Today, Ben buys time with a staff of five permanent employees in up-to-the-minute offices. (He built the two-story building himself for his own occupancy at a cost of $200,000—and it's all paid for.)

"Let me break that down for you. One girl works out all my illustrations. She is invaluable. She has the knack of thinking as I think—seeing through a case so that together we can use each other as sounding boards. Another girl does nothing but type all illustrations.

"We use IBM equipment, and we try to make the illustrations eye-catching—go all the way—spend a little money. I spend about $100 a month on folders, cellophane covers, and a number of things to make up attractive illustrations. Because—keep this in mind—we're merchandising!

"I have one person who does nothing but correspondence, that's all. I have one person who does filing. You know why? I'll drag something out of the file, but I never take time to put it back. I guess I can really create a mess, so I have one person whose major job is to put back what I take out! This girl also handles secretarial work for my office manager.

"Then I have one person—who's really my office manager but let's call him an *expediter*—a very clean-cut young man who, among other things, completes applications. Not me! He'll follow through and get the medical completed. Not me! He'll handle the million details that have to be handled in an office to take care of the amount of business we have on the books. There are many, many things—all time-consuming. He'll follow through and try to iron out whatever presents itself in the way

Planning (II)

of problems. Then the policy will come back to my desk. *He handled all the details. Not me!*

"Recently, I've added a C.P.A. part time.

"So, I have six people: Two making illustrations, one for correspondence, one for filing, an office manager-expediter, and a C.P.A. I keep them all busy."

To get the most from his office staff (and buy himself *more* time for his money), Ben applies his success-principle of scheduling. He operates his office on time-table efficiency, and that permits him to schedule his own work for greater productivity.

"At 8 o'clock in the morning, I'm in the office. At 8:30, my expediter comes in. The girls come in at 9. Then it gets pretty hectic down there. Phones start ringing—people begin coming in." But the delegation of responsibilities and the scheduling of each employee's activities pays off. By 10:30—"maybe 11:30 at the latest"—Ben is on the road.

A radio-telephone in his car links his office to him throughout the day. "If I'm not in the car when they want me, a light flicks on the dashboard, so I know they've been trying to call me. I'll pick up the radio and call them and see what they want. So we're in pretty close contact with each other regardless of where I am.

"I'll do my work, and, as a rule, I won't be back in my East Liverpool office again that day. If I'm working in the Youngstown area, I'll check back into my Youngstown office at about 6:30, and I'll be there for thirty minutes to an hour-and-a-half." And home? "Between 8 and 9 p.m. You go out to work and the first thing you know, it's night."

Making the Sale

Ben's staff gives him the time he needs. "So many of us spend time doing what can be done by a good secretary. As we go along, we become more and more knowledgeable, more and more capable. We find that we have the capacity to develop larger and larger cases, but we no longer have the time.

"Get a secretary—pick a good one—and show her what you want done. Invest in good office equipment. Delegate details to others. Spend your time doing what you can do best—*selling*."

*   *   *   *   *   *

"To be successful you must have a plan. And a plan means: A goal. It means a track to run on. And it means a schedule to save time."

And how big can you become with this plan?

"As big as you want to be," says this millionaire whose first job was that of a $10-a-week egg salesman. "Your value depends on what you make of yourself.

"Make the most of *yourself*, for that is all there is of you."

PREPARATION | 4

'Keep it simple'
'A procedure—not a problem'

You make the most of yourself—and Ben's career proves it—when you're prepared, "when you know what you're talking about, when you're *sure*."

    When Ben calls on a prospect, he *is* sure. Not simply because he prepared the day before, but because he's been preparing for that interview *every* day he's been in the business. His preparation began with a depth-knowledge of life insurance acquired by consistent day-to-day study. Even now at the peak of his career—a pinnacle no other man has ever achieved—he tops off a 12-hour-plus day ("its too short") with as much as two-hour's study. "It's his chief form of relaxation," observes an understanding wife.

"You can't compromise with knowledge. To get to know something you've got to study."

How did Ben learn to study? It was a do-it-yourself course. Born in New York City in 1912, Ben was one of nine children of Isaac and Bertha Dardick Feldman, who had fled the ghettos of Russia to find opportunity in the land of freedom. As a small boy, Ben was taken with his family to Salineville, Ohio, where his father set up a family business. "My parents bought and sold produce, cattle, hogs, chickens, eggs, and it was a case of everybody pitching in and doing his part. We were by no means well-to-do—our family was large—and my parents felt it more important for me to chip in and carry the load than it was to go to school." Because he couldn't attend classes, he had to teach himself.

Ben got through his third high school year even though he actually went to school less than an hour a week. He would pick up his assignments on Monday morning, master them in the evening after helping his father in his business. He'd deliver them completed to his teachers on Friday afternoon. He was always a good student. "I can remember a teacher coming into the room with a list of those pupils who didn't have to take the examination. She read only my name!"

"But in that senior year, I was told that I was slaughtering the attendance record. I was informed in a very nice way either come to school or don't come to school. Of course, I had no choice. I had to work."

He didn't get his high school diploma then—when he was sixteen. But he got its equivalent—nearly twenty years later when he was thirty-six. In order to start studying for a Chartered Life Underwriter's designation, basic qualifications called for at least a high school diploma. So, Ben Feldman, father of two children, already a success, went to Youngstown College at night to brush up on high school math, English and history. Then he took college entrance examinations—passed them—and the American College of Life Underwriters accepted this in lieu of that missing high school diploma.

That studying habit, picked up in his high school days, came in handy when he joined New York Life in 1942. "We had some guidance. Some of us had good managers, but the kind of training they get today was unheard of then. I studied that rate book. I would spend hours and hours with nothing but a rate book. There were all kinds of contracts in it, and I learned those contracts inside and out."

That knowledge is now an inseparable part of him. The rate book and policy contract became the foundation for Feldman's pyramiding knowledge. "You see, the rate book, basically, is just mechanics—2 plus 2 make 4. I had to make sure a policy didn't make 5; that it only made 4. But there are other things to learn—many, many things to be on top of."

When, in his third year with New York Life, he made the big leap into the Million Dollar Round Table, he set aside one or two hours each night for advanced study in programming and business and tax insurance. With his Million Dollar Round Table membership achieved, he wrote:

"Naturally, I want to become the best professional life insurance man in my area. Applied knowledge is the answer. I have started on the C.L.U. program and I'm keeping up my daily study hours. . ."

"Read!" Ben today urges. "There are so many services and bulletins coming in from my own company—publications—oh, a lot of stuff. Read! Keep reading. And you learn after a while to read more quickly, so you don't have to spend so much time reading—you can get it just by glancing."

His reading is not just limited to insurance publications. He devours any literature that could possibly boost his sales in any way. New tax developments, for example, often affect the personal and business needs of his clients, and Ben has kept himself well supplied with tax information. "Read. Study never stops because the publications never stop coming in. It's read and study. And think about *what* you're studying. Take it apart and put it together. Ask 'why?' And know the answers.

"As the years go by, you become more confident, because knowledge gives you power. You're so sure of yourself, you can build a fire under a prospect.

"Know your business well enough so you're right at home no matter what the prospect brings up."

* * * * * *

But getting ready to make a sale is not only a matter of a general preparation. In the Feldman Method, it's a highly *specific* procedure. The knowledge and *savvy* which Ben has built up so painstakingly over the years is a bit like a springboard. The procedure for preparing the sales call, and particularly the sales interview, bounds from it. It's a procedure streamlined to solve each prospect's special problems, to meet each prospect's individualized needs. And it all begins with—the problem.

Preparation

Every man has problems that only life insurance can solve. In the young man's case, the problem is to *create* cash; for the older man, to *conserve* it. There are many variations of these problems. There are many different ways of creating plans for solving these problems. These are Ben's *ideas!*

The track Ben runs on breaks his goals down into a weekly volume from a minimum of three sales. But it's the ideas that are the blueprints for the policies. What otherwise would be dull, complex actuarial legalisms are transformed into attractive "packages of money" that anyone can understand. Packages that solve a problem. Packages that do a specific job, a job the prospect needs done. Packages that solve a prospect's fundamental need for cash.

"When I began, my packages were small, because I was thinking small. An 'education' package. A 'retirement' package. They excited me. *Then!* But ideas tend to get old. Then they don't excite me any longer, and I can't run. I have the track to run on, but the motivation I need, the excitement, is gone. You've got to be enthused and excited. New ideas, bigger ideas like new goals and bigger goals make me run.

"Forever, I'm trying to find new fundamental ideas—ideas that result in *big* sales. Some come from the magazines I read. Others come from talking to people, attending insurance meetings, mulling over the notes I'm always jotting down into my little black book. Something someone says may just ring a special bell for me.

"I may take a little something from you. And from you. And from you. I'll beg it, I'll borrow it, I'll steal it, and I'll try to make it my own. I have gleaned my ideas from the minds of many men—but in return, I'll share any ideas I have with you.

Making the Sale

If you have an idea and I have an idea, and we trade ideas, no one has lost! Now we each have *two* ideas!

"You know, life insurance isn't simple, I can't understand it unless I make it simple. I figure if I can understand it, then the prospect can understand it.

"I get this idea, and I put it together and I take it apart—and I put it together and I take it apart—and I put it together and I take it apart—and I put it together and I take it apart. A thirty-second statement often takes six hours to prepare. I have three girls in my office who sometimes think I'm a little bit mixed up. It looked good. It looked all right to them. And yet I still wanted it changed. I want it the way I want it. When I have it the way I want it, then it will work."

When he feels he has it down pat, he often tries it out on his wife, Fritzie, who's been his sounding board (and his inspiration and extra source of energy) ever since he entered the life insurance business. If Fritzie approves, he knows it's a merchandisable package.

But sometimes Fritzie will say: "Ben, you're crazy!" And then, back he goes to try and rework the idea until Fritzie knows he's not fumbling or guessing—that the proposal is down to a point where Ben knew it cold—and *knew* he knew it.

The result is a masterpiece of simplicity. Ben sees every idea very plainly. He then reduces it to its most understandable terms. He sees it so clearly, and keeps it so simple, that "even a 12-year-old corporation president can understand it."

Ben forces his prospect to see his problem clearly. He must prove to his prospect that solving this problem has a price tag on it; that it will cost more to do *nothing* about it than it will to do *something* about it. He must make the prospect

Preparation

uncomfortable enough to *do* something about it. And, when the prospect has been brought to that stage, have a solution to his problem ready—a simple idea—packaged at a price the prospect can afford.

Ben develops his sales presentation as meticulously as his ideas. He spends far more time in preparation than in presentation. He has found no short cuts. A tape recorder and constant playback, reworking, makes every word mean exactly what he wants it to mean in order to carry the persuasive punch he wants it to carry. His aim again is utter clear-cut simplicity. The actual illustrations themselves follow the same pattern—they're glamorized clarity.

"We make them look good. We use special paper, modern type and color. Without exception, the girl who produces each illustration will make each one up more than once. Maybe she'll make it up several times, until it's the way I want it. Until it's simple.

"And when you're ready, the world stands still for you. When you're not—you're the unhappiest guy in the world.

"You're ready when you've followed a specific procedure to prepare you to make the sale. You see, the sale of life insurance is a procedure not a problem. It only becomes a problem when it ceases to be a procedure."

PROSPECTING | 5

'Find the man with the problem'

The track that Ben runs on demands three applications a week, and, even today, that means four, six, eight calls a day. On *whom* does he call? *Where* does he find his prospects? As with most salesmen, prospecting is always his biggest problem.

But like all other problems of selling, it can be licked by procedure—a system. In the Feldman Method, the procedure grows out of preparation. The preparation for Feldman's prospecting often begins with one of his "ideas."

"Basically, I would get all excited about an idea. I'd call it a special policy. A simple package. A policy, for example, designed to make sure a wife will never be financially dependent on her children. A policy designed to convert brick and steel back into dollars, so a family ends up with money instead of frozen assets.

"Then, when I had the idea, ready in a very simple package, I'd write down a list of people. Then I'd make up an illustration. It would be very simple—blunt—right to the point . . . and I'd know it inside and out. Then I'd begin calling on the people on my list. 'I'd like to show you something'—and the minute I'd show one of these people, just like that—I might find myself right smack in the middle of an interview."

Where do the names come from?

Suppose he wants to know who's who in the Ajax Company. First thing he'll do is get a Dun & Bradstreet report. He wants to find out how big they are. He wants to find out if they have life insurance. He wants to find out what they own, what they owe, are they growing, and how fast. One thing he finds out is the name of the President—Mr. Doakes. Then he finds out something about Mr. Doakes.

"How? You know most of our companies have been around a long time. Somewhere, someone may have written him a policy in New York Life. I'd like to know. I'd be pretty stupid, you know, if I called on him and I didn't know this. So I take that name—Mr. Doakes—and ask our Central Service: 'Do we have any coverage on this man? And if so, may I please have a brief.' It's amazing the 'orphan' cases you sometimes find! [Ed. note: In insurance selling vernacular, an 'orphan' case refers to a company policyholder who, because he's moved to another part of the country or for some other reason, is no longer serviced by his original life insurance agent.]

Prospecting

"But assume no coverage with us! All I know is the size of the company—that they don't have much cash—that they've been growing—and that it looks as if Mr. Doakes controls the company. It looks as though it's a one-man company, and he's the one. So we go from there. 'Mr. Doakes, I'd like to show you something. . .' "

Since most of Ben's cases center around solving the cash problems of businesses and estates, he looks for men of means who have little liquid cash. He looks for a man who has no money—but one who has wealth, usually a business, often property or any assortment of assets. But this man, even though he shows a fine balance sheet, rarely has much cash.

In addition Ben has his "blotter list" of about 300 key people. He sends each man a blotter every month. In these days of fast-drying ink, few people use blotters, but Ben doesn't mind. He's concerned with getting his name in front of the prospect in an attractive way, and he believes the blotter does it. On this list, he may have a half-dozen people in steel fabrication, half a dozen people manufacturing storm doors, half a dozen people in this kind of plant, doing this kind of work—all kinds of people in all kinds of industry.

The prospect's name is printed on the front of the blotter, and his own name on the blotting side—'Ben Feldman representing New York Life. Planned Insurance Estates, Member of the Million Dollar Round Table.' And then his address. It's simple and it works!

"Most of the people on my blotter list are, I might say, 'centers of influence,' and I'm forever visiting them for more names. I send them an informal letter twice a year reporting on my activities—my results. Somebody said: 'Put yourself on record.' I do, with a letter saying I have done 'so and so,' or I hope to do 'so and so.' It's surprising how much pride they take in my being their insurance man. They're willing to give me information. They're willing to talk about people. It works!

"I also screen names that I read about, names that I hear about in casual conversation, and names referred to me from sources other than the blotter list. Almost all names are residents of my community.

"All my business—I'd say 90 percent of it—comes from my home town of about 22,000 people, and from Youngstown, about 40 miles away, with 175,000 people; or from the area between the two. To go beyond this is to waste time—I've only 24 hours a day, not 48. I don't want to spend two hours just going someplace. That's a lot of lost motion. Maybe the case has a good potential, nevertheless the day is wrecked. I used to float around quite a bit—but not any more. You can talk to people in your own back yard, or you can look for people hundreds of miles away. I'd rather stay in my own back yard."

All the people Ben screens as prospects have one thing in common: a problem that can be solved by life insurance. He looks for that man with the problem. He looks for men with a problem his ideas can solve.

When he knows something in advance about the man—as with Mr. Doakes of Ajax Company—he selects an idea from his repertory of simple packages that he feels will solve this man's specific problem. When he cannot uncover the man's problem in advance, he tries to turn "the suspect into a prospect" with dramatically disturbing questions that serve as probes.

"So far he's just a name, so first I like to drive by and see this man, meet him for just a few minutes. Sometimes, I may

Prospecting

ask him; 'I'm looking for a job, will you hire me? I'll work for less than your lowest paid office clerk—but I'll pay your taxes.'

"The man's response will usually show me whether he has a tax problem that one of my packaged ideas will solve. Or I may ask him: 'How would you like to insure one year's profits?' It's a provocative opener to the idea of 'keyman insurance'—and the man's reaction should quickly tell me whether a keyman's loss would hurt the suspect's business."

With the disturbing question, Feldman has found a powerful technique for identifying problems. Each disturbing question—or each group of related disturbing questions—refers to a specific problem.

"But people have so many problems! You know what the young man's problem is? He hasn't had the time to accumulate his estate, so we have to create one. The older man's problem? He's been successful. He's made a lot of money. You know what his problem is? To conserve the money he has made! Over the years, I've refined these disturbing questions so each will strike with maximum power:

> *Would you like to create a guaranteed market for your company?*
>
> *or*
>
> *How much time would it take to repay everything you owe? How much is that time worth to you?*
>
> *or*
>
> *Tell me, what's the most valuable thing you've got? Your company? Want it to continue? Could you run your company without money?*

or

Would you say six percent would be a fair return on money? Well, Uncle Sam is going to take 30 —40—maybe 50 percent.

or

Did you ever have a problem, or does everything run smoothly?

or

Would you like to buy your partner's interest for pennies on the dollar?

or

Why pay your taxes out of principal?

With the aid of these and other disturbing questions, Feldman is able to pin down the prospect's problem. Prospecting for him is recognizing the problem and making sure that problem has a price tag.

"There's a price tag on doing nothing about his problem, and there's a price tag on doing something. But the price tag for doing nothing is far greater than the price tag for doing something. The problem means nothing unless the man *wants* to do something about it. The price tag makes him *want* to."

Even though Ben has already recognized the problem— even if he knows of a man's problem *in advance*—he still uses the disturbing question. *When it shakes the man*, he knows he has a *bona fide* prospect.

But disturbing questions do more than serve as a tool for *active* prospecting. They do more than just identify a prospect. They open the door to the solution—to the presentation of the

Prospecting

idea. For the answers to the questions *are* the answers to the man's problems. As the interview progresses, through carefully conceived disturbing questions, the answers become the idea—the clear-cut simple package that he sells.

Ben's disturbing questions are so phrased that they pinpoint the problem and make the prospect very uncomfortable. Ben shows him that it's *his* problem, that the solution has a price tag on it, that someone will have to pay it. If it isn't too late—if the prospect can still qualify—Ben will suggest the prospect may be able to pay for it with "discounted dollars."

"Let's find out. I'll put it together and you take a look. All I need is medical underwriting. I'll set up an appointment with our doctor that is convenient for you. Give me two or three weeks and I'll be back!"

Prospecting, then, is a relatively simple procedure: Conceive the idea and bring it to the man whose problem it will solve. Or find a man with a problem, and bring the problem-solving idea to him. In either case, you've found, not just a name, but a prospect. Or, as Ben puts it, "Prospecting is nothing but people and ideas."

THE CALL | 6

'I just walk in'

Before Ben can bring people and ideas together, he must get *in* to see the people. He must make calls. Not just *a* call now and then—but regular calls! "Obviously," you say. Nevertheless it's a fundamental of salesmanship many agents, and especially the successful ones, sometimes seem to forget.

"You know, you get to the point where you're so good, you think you know everything. You think—'I've made a lot of calls, I've got a lot of programs, a lot of prospects—I can sit in my office, and get on the phone and call some of these people.' It's so wrong. After a while, you're not writing any volume.

You're not selling when you're sitting in your office. It doesn't work that way.

"Fundamentals are right down to earth. And one fundamental is: You have to make calls. *Nothing* happens until you make a call. It's that fundamental!"

Today Ben Feldman averages between 30 and 40 calls a week. Whom he calls on is determined by his prospecting procedure. Occasionally he has made a pinpoint use of a third person letter as a door-opener to prepare a few carefully selected people for his call.

The Call

Early one fall, Ben made a list of 30 small corporation presidents or owners of large sole proprietorships and asked a company officer to sign and send the following pre-approach letters, at the rate of one a day over the following month:

```
Dear Mr. Baker:

    Keymen can make or break a company.
They are directly responsible for profits
and losses.

    New York Life has a plan designed to
do for you what your keymen do -- make
money.  We could guarantee that, if your
keyman is "called out of the picture"...

    ONE MILLION TAX-FREE DOLLARS COULD
BE CALLED IN!

    The cost is surprisingly low to those
who can qualify.  Won't you give our very
able sales representative, Mr. Ben Feldman,
the courtesy of an interview to explain
how he has set up such a plan for many
Eastern Ohio businesses?

                        Sincerely,


                        A. H. Thomson
                        Vice President
```

Results: $7,000,000 in new sales!

Making the Sale

Here's a second:

Dear Mr. Jones:

Taxes tend to create problems - income taxes for you while you live - estate taxes for your heirs when you are gone.

Especially in recent years, New York Life has issued million dollar policies designed for purposes of "discounting" estate taxes. We have asked Mr. Ben Feldman to visit you with a similar proposal for your consideration. He has been with New York Life for more than twenty-five years, and is extremely well qualified in this field.

Actually, very few people can qualify for a policy of this amount. In the past 20 years, New York Life has placed less than 100 such policies on the books and Mr. Feldman has written many of them. We would appreciate your extending him the courtesy of an interview.— No obligation, of course!

Sincerely yours,

A. H. Thomson
Vice-President

And a third:

Dear Mr. Prout:

Here's an idea for the man with big problems! ONE MILLION DOLLARS -- TAX FREE -- to your company!

The day your keyman "walks out" ...

ONE MILLION DOLLARS WALKS IN!

New York Life Insurance Company, nearly 125 years old -- with many billions on the books -- still has fewer than 200 "Million Dollar Plans" in force.

Very few men can qualify for such a plan!

Won't you give our very able representative, Mr. Ben Feldman, the courtesy of an interview to explain how such a plan might serve you?

                        Sincerely,

                        A. H. Thomson
                        Vice-President

Making the Sale

Ben uses these third-party letters sparingly, but with startling effect. Like his approach, these letters have been honed to a razor-edge of striking power.

(One September, 28 letters like the one to Mr. Jones were sent to business owners. Ben got in to see 21 of them; had honest-to-goodness interviews with 12 of them; closed seven and delivered $8,500,000 before the end of the same year.)

Here's a letter Ben himself sends:

Dear Mr. Sims:

If you had died during the past year, who would have paid the inheritance tax -- your lawyer, your auditor, or your family?

Could they have paid it for $10 a day? Could they even have borrowed the money and paid the interest for $10 a day?

Put me on your payroll for $10 a day and I'll pay what must be paid.

Respectfully,

Ben Feldman, C.L.U.

The Call

Here's another of Ben's letters—his "Lookback Letter" for policy owner changes:

Dear Mr. Arnold:

   Will you trade..............

   One hour of your time for $1.00 each day for the rest of your life?

   On July 14th, your insurance rate goes up $1.00 per day forever.

   Best wishes.

                              Ben Feldman, C.L.U.

He looks in his birthday book every month, and sends as many as twenty such letters—*with a crisp dollar bill pinned to each one!*

Does this pre-conditioning by a different type of letter and personalized blotters, pay off? The proof is in the results: "These cases run into six—even seven figures," says Ben.

* * * * * *

"These letters tell the prospect to expect me . . . and I don't think I make more than two calls to get a good interview. Most of my calls are made without even telephoning ahead to set up an appointment. I rarely use the telephone because . . . well, he may not want to see me! I have a better chance of

Making the Sale

seeing the man I want to see if I *do* go! Besides, switchboard girls and secretaries have become very good. They've learned to take you apart. 'Who? Why? What for? What company?' You don't always get by. I seldom call on the phone. I'd rather go.

"If you do use the telephone, make the best possible use of it. Plan the words you are going to use. Know exactly *what* you are going to say. Say it—and hang up!

"On calls, I just walk in—and my first barrier is usually the switchboard operator or the receptionist. On the phone, a switchboard operator can stop me dead. But face to face, the odds are I'll get by! And when I go, I may leave something with her. You know what it is? It's a pair of little golden slippers. She doesn't know what they are until I've left and she's opened the box. Then I usually get a thank you note. From that time on, I can get in.

"I'm very frank, very open. I just say I want to meet her boss, whatever his name might be. (And you'd better know his name!) The receptionist ordinarily announces me, but it's a cold call, and the odds are he doesn't want to see me. I get thrown out of more places! As many places as anyone. I don't mean physically.

"There are so many ways of saying, 'No.' He probably won't see me the first time. That isn't so bad. Why? Because I'm coming back, and when I come back I'm no longer a stranger! I've been here before!"

"Even the girl will recognize me next time I come back. I carry a special celluloid calendar business card. Why? Because it's a little bit different. When you hand this to the girl—it's a little bit different than the cards she received yesterday and the other cards she receives today. She'll remember me.

The Call

"And, if I call once or twice more, and if the answer is still 'No,' she'll probably begin to feel sorry for me. Now she's on my team. She'll do her best to open the door for me. Particularly if she feels I'd be helping her boss. You've got to have disturbing things to say to the receptionist that will make her boss want to see you, just as you have disturbing things to say to the boss himself."

Sometimes it's extremely difficult to get in even with a receptionist won over. Then Ben does something a bit more startling. Once he simply couldn't get in to see a man who was the highest on his company's payroll. So he sent in five brand-new $100-bills with a note that said: "I'll trade these for five minutes." It worked! If it hadn't, Feldman might never have had a chance to create that $2,500,000 case. And no one yet has ever kept one of those bills.

"Sooner or later, the prospect will see me—if only long enough to brush me off! Most men are courteous. They'll see you. But he may not let me into his office. You know what he *will* do? He'll come out. What he wants to do is get rid of you. So you try to sense: 'Is he in a hurry? Does he want to brush you off?' You try to go along with the prospect's mood. You say 'Hello' and that you just wanted to meet him. You tell him you'd like to stop back. Don't ask for a date. Say: 'You don't mind if I stop back, do you?' Usually he won't say, 'No.'

"This brief encounter is followed up with a thank you note . . . a little brochure—not to his office, to his home. And I *go* back. The point is: I don't telephone back. I *go* back. And it does work."

When Ben goes back, he's *prepared*. Most calls, you'll remember, are not really cold calls. The prospect may know nothing about Ben, but Ben has found out a lot about the pros-

Making the Sale

pect. Now on a true cold call the same fact-finding procedures are put to work. He picks up bits and pieces of pertinent information about the prospect. How old is he? What does he earn? Who are his key people? Is he expanding? What's his role in the corporate structure? What kind of business is he a part of? Is he wealthy? Are his assets frozen?

"If I want to sell to someone in the XYZ Corporation, and I see it's steel fabrication, I'll go back to someone who operates in that same field who may already be a policyholder. 'What do you know about Ajax? About Mr. Doakes?' And I can find out a lot. How much he owes, how much he owns. It won't be all the information I'll need, but I'll get some idea of his problem. 'How big is he?' A Dun & Bradstreet report will give me an idea how big. I make lots of cold calls like any other salesman but the second time I see a man, he's no longer a stranger.

"Every man has a problem. Simply look for the problem. When you've found it—and make darned sure that you have *found* it—that you recognize it—that you understand it so well that you know the price of doing *something* about it and the price of doing *nothing* about it—when you know all that—then *communicate*.

"How? There should be questions. Clear-cut questions—questions thought out beforehand to make a man think. Isaac Kibrick (a great life insurance salesman), always said: 'Look for the loss,' and that's what I probe for with disturbing questions. When you start a man thinking about money—about his loss—you're making him uncomfortable, you're lighting a fire under him."

Ben's investigation uncovered the prospect's vulnerable spots, and now in his easy, quiet way, he continues to slash at

The Call

them painfully with his questions, the same kind of razor-edged questions that work so successfully in active prospecting.

Ben never studied Freud but he agrees with the famed psychiatrist who said that "once you understand the problem you can deal with it."

"I pinpoint a man's problems. For example, I'll say:

> You spent thirty years putting this company together. I've never known anybody who had a lease on life; do you? No? Then it's only a question of time until you walk out and Uncle Sam walks in. Know what he wants? Money! And he has a way of getting it. First. Not last. Could you, right now, give me 30 percent of everything you own—in cash—that's the least Uncle Sam will take—without it hurting a little bit? Do you think it would affect your credit position? Your working position?

"Pinpoint his loss. Light a bonfire under him. Explain a very simple fact of financial security—that there's a price tag on doing something. And there's a price tag on doing nothing. The price tag on doing nothing comes a lot higher in the end. *Make him uncomfortable enough to do something about his problem.* And when he reaches that point—when he realizes he ought to do something to prevent his loss—be prepared with the idea that will solve his problem.

> You spend a lifetime locking money up in bricks and stone and steel. Someday, someone will have to unlock those bricks and convert them back into money. Wouldn't it be easier to hire me for $10 a day and let me do this for you? The day you walk out, $100,000 walks in.

"If I can find the answer to his problem . . . we're communicating."

Ben says: "I'm a package salesman, but there is a solid tax idea behind my package and I dress it up in emotional needs."

*   *   *   *   *   *

The sole objective of the approach—from the decision to call to the disturbing questions—is to set up an interview. At first it's a call . . . nothing but a call. But if the prospect's receptive—if Ben has been able to communicate—Ben will be back. And when he comes back, it's an interview.

THE INTERVIEW I : ATTITUDE 7

'First "buy" it—then you'll sell it'

The key to the sale is the interview and Ben is prepared for it. He's pinpointed the problem. He's come up with the problem-solving idea. He's merchandised it into a package so simple that the prospect can grasp it quickly and easily. He's ready—*logically*.

But he knows logic isn't enough to persuade his prospect. The appeal is not only to the brain but to the heart. The prospect must sense Ben's sincerity—feel his excitement! He must be caught up in his enthusiasm. The prospect must not only believe *what* Ben is telling him—he must believe in *Ben*.

How does Ben create this confidence?

Making the Sale

"Your biggest asset is a positive mental attitude. If you decide you are going to feel wonderful, strong, excited—then you have the power to move mountains. You begin to get this feeling when you know that through your knowledge of life insurance you can help another human being. I get wrapped up in these cases, and I'm not just trying to make another dollar. Things are very, very real to me. So real. I see the problem through the prospect's eyes and make it my own. The most important person to disturb and get steamed up in the interview is me."

When Ben is certain that he holds the solution to the man's problem in his hands, everything he does projects confidence—naturally. The way he sits. His smile. His gestures. The way he looks at the prospect. Confidence becomes as much a part of him as his breathing. Quiet, self-assured confidence. Never a trace of high-pressure selling.

Ben is *sure* that because of his answer, of his solution, a man's business won't fall apart, a family will stay together, a widow won't have to shoulder heavy burdens at an advanced age—and from that certainty, as a matter of course, his *self*-assurance follows.

But Ben's natural confidence—so much a part of him that it's been called his trademark—has very deep roots. He could not be convinced he holds the solution to a man's problems unless he were first convinced of the value of life insurance itself.

"I remember—this goes back quite a little way," Ben tells this story of his early days as a life insurance agent. "There was this dentist. Drafted into World War II. He had two youngsters—and he was conscious of what life insurance meant,

THE INTERVIEW (I): ATTITUDE

and he wanted it. But when he came back from the war, his practice had fallen apart—he had no money.

"A problem. I had to have a solution. So I worked out a plan for him by which he would give me a dollar a day—just a dollar a day. And he actually put that dollar a day aside—every day. And at first I'd even go to his office every Saturday and actually pick up those dollars he had put aside one by one, day by day.

"And, you know, a short time later, he came down with polio. In just a few months he was gone. And you know something—

"The biggest thing he left his wife was the return on that one dollar a day. It meant *everything* to that man's family—*everything*.

"And it made a tremendous impact on me.

"I began to realize what it means when you read the front page of a policy. 'We promise to pay. . . .' What? 'The face amount of the policy. . . .' When? 'Immediately upon proof of death.'

"I began to understand this tremendous thing we have for sale. We're *underwriting your tomorrows*. How much are they worth? How much are your tomorrows worth? How much are they worth to you? How much are they worth to your family without you? 'We promise to pay. . . .' When? *Immediately!* Something like this tends to make you believe. . . .

"This was my first death claim and, for the first time, I began to understand the fundamental purpose of life insurance was . . .

Making the Sale

To create cash. The stock market is where money makes money. But life insurance creates cash where none had existed before. The basic purpose of life insurance is to create. A piece of paper, a drop of ink and pennies on the dollar . . . and we can create more than most men can accumulate.

The best investment in the world is the one that pays the most when you need it the most—and that's life insurance.

"Had my dentist friend lived, he could have accumulated money for his family. He had the ability. But what he ran out of was time. Life insurance underwrites time."

Ability is the one thing that you alone can furnish. But also you must have *time*. No matter how much ability you have, you cannot accomplish what you want unless you have time to finish. If I could guarantee that you would live 10 . . . or 20 . . . or 30 years more—how much would you be willing to pay for that time?

The uncertain factor in success is time. Life insurance is time—the time a man might not have. If he needs time, he needs life insurance.

Later, as Ben became increasingly interested in estate planning, he made great use of life insurance's unique ability to create cash that can conserve the money a man has accumulated over a lifetime.

The act of dying creates a problem. Part of what you own isn't yours. The government is going to take it away from you in the form of

The Interview (I): Attitude

taxes. Wouldn't you—for just pennies a day—be willing to protect those hard-earned dollars?

"Life insurance is the only tool that costs pennies and guarantees dollars. It's a tool that's designed to create and then to conserve. It puts foundations beneath men's plans. It underwrites that element of time.

"It's like the machine designed to do a certain specific kind of work—and nothing in the world will take its place. Most men hold very close to their hearts the welfare of those they love. They want to be sure. But when a man tries to substitute for life insurance, he eliminates certainty. No substitute can get the job done. There *is* no substitute for life insurance!"

Ben tells of a company he knew that had received a million-dollar order. The order could be fulfilled only by one keyman in that company, and he was asked by the president to get examined for life insurance. But he kept putting it off and before it could be completed, the keyman died.

"Life insurance would have guaranteed continuity for that company, continuity for all the people depending on the company, self-respect and security for the man's family. There was no way in the world this could have been done except with this sort of tool. But he waited—and all this went down the drain.

"That's why I can never take 'no' for an answer when I'm sure a man needs life insurance. I worked on one case for about a year. It was with a doctor who had been examined for life insurance, and, in the company's opinion, he had a serious medical impairment. He was a physician himself and disagreed with our findings. But he needed insurance. The bulk of his estate was basically his home, Series E bonds, and a little bit of

Making the Sale

cash. I called a number of times, but made no progress, until late one evening we finally agreed on a $50,000 very highly-rated contract. It was none too soon. Within two months, the man had a massive heart attack and died. The life insurance proved to be a life saver for his family.

"There were other cases like the doctor's and the keyman's. All pretty much alike. And they make you realize what you are doing is so tremendous because it's doing a lot of good for a lot of people. And, remember, life insurance has been around for a long, long time. It didn't start yesterday. It's been here for 200 years. And everything about it is good. It does good for so many people. It makes you realize that what you're doing is really very worthwhile."

It is in this realization—based on an understanding of the purpose and potentials of life insurance—that one finds the roots of Ben's unshakable confidence. When he began to sell life insurance, he was afraid, scared. But when he got to the point where he was convinced that what he was doing was good for the other man, then he wasn't afraid. Since he was trying to help the man he was calling on, he surely didn't have to apologize for being helpful. He wasn't hurting him by taking his money. He was helping him.

These roots of confidence have always been fed by study. Life insurance, he knew, was a powerful tool for helping people, but he had to learn how to use that tool skillfully to help his prospects solve their *specific* problems. In his rate book are about 30 different types of policies. Each is actuarially and mathematically sound. But they don't *fit* every situation. His self-imposed task was to learn which ones did fit and how to adapt them.

The Interview (I): Attitude

"So I would spend hour after hour with a rate book. Just a rate book, pencil and paper until I knew the rate book inside out. Tell me why Paid Up at 65 is better or worse than Whole Life. Why shouldn't it be 10-Pay Life? Why shouldn't it be Retirement at 60 or something like that? I had to know *why* . . . I had to know what to answer when a man said to me, '*What if* . . . ?' no matter what that 'if' was . . .

"So I was able to fit each policyholder like a tailor fits a suit from a bolt of cloth. If you wanted to buy a suit, you wouldn't close your eyes, would you, and grab a suit? You'd want someone to fit you. If you walked in to buy a pair of shoes, you wouldn't buy *any* pair. You'd try to have someone fit you. It's not enough just to know everything that goes into making up a life insurance contract. You've got to understand where and when to apply them.

"For the most part, I rely on Whole Life. I believe we can do more with Whole Life than anything else in the rate book. Whole Life is so flexible, there's hardly anything you can't do with it."

When Ben steps into an interview, he knows he has measured his prospect. He *knows*, too, that none of the prospect's objections or questions are going to impede the interview. Years of intensive and continuous study of all aspects of life insurance have converted Ben's brain into the memory bank of a computer: he's ready with the answers instantly. He *knows*. And because he knows, his confidence is strengthened. He feels certain, enthusiastic, excited, strong—and his whole body projects this attitude. Ben is a quiet, gentle man, but the prospect feels the impact of that certainty as forcefully as he feels the wallop of Ben's power phrases.

Making the Sale

"The prospect knows from the way you sit, the way you look at him, particularly the way you *say something*, that you're *sure*—for what is enthusiasm except the excitement in your voice? It's not so much what you say as how you say it. Speak slowly, clearly, softly—but definitely—and your enthusiasm, your sincerity, will carry over. Once you're sure of yourself, it'll show—all over! He'll *know* that *you* know what you're saying, what you're talking about, and that what you're talking about is good for him. Your attitude carries conviction.

"And you build that attitude by being *sure!* First, in your own mind, you've got to buy it. First 'buy' it—and then you'll sell it. But—if *you* don't 'buy' it first, you'll *never* sell it!"

*   *   *   *   *   *

If Ben Feldman's sales messages convey sincerity, it's because they *are* sincere. He knows that the problems he sets out to solve for his clients can be solved by one tool, and one tool alone—"that tremendous instrument, life insurance." It's a conviction that gives him his persuasive self-confidence, and something more: a single-mindedness and an almost evangelical zeal toward all aspects of his work. Ben's belief in life insurance makes Ben's clients believe in him. He's *sure*.

THE INTERVIEW
II : PRESENTATION

8

'The disturbing question is the key'

"When you enter an interview *sure* that you've recognized the prospect's problem, *sure* that you've found the solution for it, then your own attitude is *sure* to create a psychological atmosphere conducive to success."

This attitude is at the heart of Ben Feldman's great personal appeal. A humble and basically shy man, he is the very opposite of the popular conception of the hail-fellow-well-met, glamor-type salesman. But in an interview he radiates a contagious confidence and enthusiasm that captures the mind of his prospect. It's an attitude that *can* be developed, as he has developed it, by continuous study and unrelenting hard work, by

Making the Sale

painstaking preparation, and by an unswerving belief in the product he sells.

His interviews are anything but "canned" sales talks. He knows his product so well, and he understands his prospect's problems so intimately, that his knowledge becomes simple conversation. It's one man talking to another. It's the friendly give-and-take between one man with a problem and another man who sincerely wants to help him solve it. It becomes an interchange of ideas.

"I believe in a man's problems—but I've still got to lead him along," says Ben. "The key to the sale is the interview. But remember—*remember*—the key to the interview is the *disturbing question*."

Lillian Hogue, a successful life insurance agent in her own right, and the only woman ever to head The American Society of Chartered Life Underwriters, makes the following comments about Feldman's style:

"Ben has discovered the immense drama of his beautiful pauses, and the art of phrasing a declarative sentence in the form of a question. An example? Ben was asked from the audience at a seminar: 'What do you say in an interview when the prospect tells you he intends to *buy term and invest the difference?*' To many life underwriters, such a statement might call for a lengthy discourse, punctuated with a red-flag array of facts, figures, and guesses, which cement more firmly the prospect's wisdom in following his own intention.

"How did Ben handle it? There was no rush of words, merely a simple, declarative sentence in the tantalizing form of a question, dramatically heightened with superb pauses:

64

The Interview (II): Presentation

" 'Term insurance is temporary insurance?.......... but the problem? .... is permanent?' .... and he gently proceeded with the interview.

"True, 'Term insurance is temporary insurance' is a declarative sentence but, when phrased with the voice lifting to a question, followed by a beautiful pause, the prospect's intelligence has not been insulted.

"Of course, Ben knows something about term insurance. He is not called upon to make an oral answer but, in his own mind, there is no point of disagreement. Then Ben continues:

" 'But the problem? .... is permanent .... ?' The prospect's own unique problem is suddenly emphasized, with another dramatic pause to refresh his memory. And those final words, 'is permanent' carry a peculiar connotation of the inexorable passage of time. No argument. No loss of face. If we just have the self-discipline, Ben's soft-sell method is there for the borrowing."

Disturbing questions in Ben's hands have become one of the most powerful tools in the history of salesmanship. They're uncanny mixtures of reason and emotion carefully developed over the years to reveal a man's financial sore spot and heal it simultaneously—to diagnose a financial ill and suggest the cure. They're probes, needles, shocks of cold water to help a man see his own problem clearly—often for the first time. Then the man *wants* to do something about it because he knows he *can* do something about it. A whip and a carrot at the same time, disturbing questions are the motivational devices which hold the key to Ben's many millions of insurance-sales volume with each passing year.

When Ben asks: "*What would you say if I told you I want 30% of everything you have in this world—and I want it now and in cash?*," he is forcing his prospect to come face to face with the tax that will hit his estate once he is dead. The question is more than disturbing, it's painful.

That probe has touched a universal, sensitive nerve. No man wants to lose valuable possessions that may have taken him a lifetime to accumulate. But, he *will* lose them, he knows it now, unless something is done about it. And something *can* be done about it.

> How would you like to put me on your payroll for less than you pay your newest clerk. And when you walk out, a hundred thousand dollars walk in?

And at such a low price compared with the price tag his executor would face if he didn't do anything about it, now, the prospect will usually *act*. The disturbing questions have activated him.

When dealing with a young man, for instance—when the problem is to create cash and not to conserve it—the disturbing question is used incisively. The one argument, the one thing that most touches his problem, that hurts him, is selected.

> Your child may have a right to a good education, but you'll need money to exercise that right. Do you have a lease on life? Do you know anyone who has a lease on life? How much time do you need to complete your plans?

Ben says: "I'm trying to hurt him, because if I don't, he's going to hurt somebody else. I try to influence a young man's life in the proper direction. It's more important than the sale of anything else." But as Ben hurts, he heals. He puts his man on the spot and then offers to lift him off.

The Interview (II): Presentation

Do you want your little boy to go to school? It isn't the policy that costs money, it's the education that costs money. May I talk to you about doing something about it? Which is cheaper, paying for your child's education in four years—or in 18 years? You have 18 years to pay for his education—if you begin *now*. You *can't* begin now? Then you'll have to pay for it all at once! Tell me—could you—right now—pay for his first year of college?

The young man's reason tells him he can't, but to put to rest the emotional turmoil Ben's questions have stirred up within him, the young man will *act*. The disturbing questions again did the activating.

*   *   *   *   *   *

"Keep the presentation simple not only for the customer's benefit, but for your own, as well. If it's simple you'll be able to present it more effectively because you'll understand it.

"Ever look at a rate book? You know there are all kinds of policies, all kinds of tables, all kinds of premiums. Hand a prospect a rate book and tell him he can have whatever he wants. What would he buy? Or would he buy anything? I don't think so. Why? He wouldn't understand. My job is to make him understand which I do with simple packages designed to do a specific job.

"My job is to merchandise—to make up simple packages! To give them names. 'Special Policy Designed to Create Cash for Your Company.' 'Special Policy Designed to Guarantee Payroll for One Year.' 'Special Policy to Discount Your Estate Tax.' The prospect is more apt to understand this than the mechanics of a contract.

"I usually sell something specific—like a special policy for John Jones designed to take care of estate taxes on his half-million dollar estate—a simple cleancut package!"

What are the price tags on Ben's packages? "Human life —what's it worth?" He might answer with a story. "A farmer out in Iowa who raised hogs, sold a load and was taking them to market. The truck stalled at a crossing just as a train was coming. The truck was destroyed, most of the hogs were destroyed. The farmer was killed. The truck and the hogs were insured. But not the farmer. Tell me, what is a man's life worth? Is anyone really over-insured? The price tags are high!"

Ben makes no little plans. He knows his prospect's problem inside and out, and he knows how *much* insurance (never how little insurance) will solve it. Ben's biggest policy owners now have $16,250,000 life insurance. But Ben isn't happy because he thinks this client has a potential $25,000,000 problem—and that, as his agent, he's been remiss in solving only part of it.

Included in Ben's clientele are more than 300 men and women who own more than $100,000 of protection. There are 40 families who have bought some $150,000,000 life insurance through him. And one client describes him as, "one hell of a salesman." And why not? That particular client's sights were raised from zero to $5,000,000!

But Ben didn't try to raise the sights of his prospects when he first began selling as an agent for New York Life. He had trouble converting over from thinking small as he did in debit selling. His ideas were small—education packages . . .

The Interview (II): Presentation

housewife packages . . . victory packages . . . and the price tags on them couldn't be much smaller. He sold a lot of $500 policies because that was the minimum. His sales approaches were built around saving 10 cents a day, maybe a quarter a day. And once in a while, $10 a month. Ben says today:

"I was afraid of a man I had to look up to. They were small policies because I was afraid to think big. But you know, it's a strange thing, maybe it's something hard to understand, but the biggest problem in the world for me and I suspect you, too, is to sell ourselves. Most men are afraid to think big. So they exchange a lifetime for very little. You exchange *your* lifetime for much too little.

"Did you ever think back: 'Gee, if only I had it to do over again!' What went wrong? We're afraid. Afraid to think big. Afraid somebody will laugh at us, make fun of us, or maybe we're just frightened. We surround ourselves with reasons and after a while we start to believe them. We're afraid. We're afraid to think big.

"How do you think big? How? Build up your own life insurance program. How big is big? Build it up and up. And this will raise your sights. Then you can raise the other man's sights.

"One thing I did every year for many years was to buy a little more life insurance for myself. So that if I had $200,000 and he had $100,000, I wasn't afraid of him. You see, I could look right *at* him, and not *up* to him. If I knew he should have more, I didn't care if he could or couldn't afford more, I knew he should have more.

"You know, it's a funny thing. If you're insured for $100,000, or insured for $200,000, you think a little bigger. When you move it up to $300,000, you hold your head a little bit higher.

Making the Sale

You move it on up, you think a little bigger. It works. It's odd, but it does work.

"There's a kind of a rule of thumb that says an agent will sell as much life insurance per month as he owns himself. I have $1,400,000 on myself, plus $300,000 on each of the boys; and another $200,000 on Fritzie. I'm putting over $1,000 a week into premiums."

There's no greater proof of a life insurance man's belief in his own product than his purchase of it in large quantities himself. Ben frequently displays his own program as an illustration. ("When you show your prospect you own the product, this will increase his confidence in insurance and also in you.") Ben can sell in millions because he's sold himself a million plus. He's not afraid of a big price tag. Nor is the prospect when it's put to him as only Ben can do it. He's more likely to feel complimented—to be flattered. How does Ben approach the client?

What's your life worth? Well, I don't know what your life's worth, but I'll make this deal with you: I'd like to hire you to work for me. I'm going to pay you exactly what you're worth *right* now. Not the price *I* put on you but the price *you* put on yourself. Whatever you've insured your life for, that's what it's worth. Would you work for me for the rest of your life for the amount of insurance on your life? Probably not, because all your tomorrows are worth more than that.

Ben was asked not long ago: "You were writing $5,000,000 a dozen years ago, and now with the same effort, the same three applications a week, you've written $40 to $50,000,000

The Interview (II): Presentation

the last couple of years. What do you think is the difference between then and now?"

"I try to think bigger. The size of the case is governed by your thinking. Think big and your case will be big. My cases get bigger because I think bigger. And then I try to stretch my prospects' minds...."

In the interview, then, Ben tries to stretch his prospect's mind with new ideas. He does this first by stretching his own mind. ("It's stretching that develops our potential, increases our ability.") He thinks big because he has become big: he's built up his own life insurance program to the point where he's proud to display it. He's no longer afraid to prescribe a package with a large price tag on it, if the prospect needs it to solve his problem. He then presents an often staggering price tag in such a way as to be a genuine compliment to the man's value. Ben has made his prospect think bigger—by first thinking bigger himself. And Ben eliminates any residual objections to price with:

> It costs *nothing* if you do, and it may cost a lifetime of effort if you don't. It costs you nothing if you do because the worst that can happen is that you'll wind up with some paid-up insurance. If you *don't* do it—well, you know things do happen. Sometimes the highest price in the world is—doing nothing. A lot of men do nothing wrong. They do nothing. And that's what's wrong. The cost of a life insurance policy *increases* each year if you *don't* have it, and *decreases* if you *do* have it. Paying the premium isn't the problem. Paying the premium is the *solution* to the problem.

But where's the money to come from to pay premiums? Ben feels he must help his prospects find it. He's already helped the man by pinpointing his problem and finding a solution; and the man is "sold" *in principle:* but there's no real sale until cash is paid so Ben goes one step further and shows him where to find the money.

"The man tells you, 'It's wonderful. Sure, I'd like to have it, but I can't afford it. I have no money.' Well, nobody has any. If you're looking for *extra* money," Ben advises his fellow salesmen, "that's wrong. There isn't any. What you have to do is help him find the money. And you can do it. The prospect does not necessarily need more *money* to do what you want him to do. The money is already there. When the chips are down, most men have a system of priorities and will put first things first."

Before going any further Ben wants to find out *if* his prospect can qualify for life insurance and for how much?

Throughout the interview, Ben's manner has been humble, gentle, soft-spoken, courteous, understanding, sympathetic—even comforting: an attitude of service and humility has established a genuine rapport between agent and prospect. It has enabled Ben to lead the prospect gently ("Never push. Don't back a man into a corner to make him say, 'Yes.' Lead him—use implied consent.")

But with the unrelenting use of disturbing questions, Ben has continued to build fires under the prospect. The man knows he has a problem. He has been offered a feasible solution. Deep down, he's a bit uncomfortable—and anxious to do something—anything to relieve this feeling. It's then that Ben says something like—

Before we go ahead, let's see if you qualify. You know that a man in business spends more ime

The Interview (II): Presentation

with business than he does with his family. As the years go by, Mother Nature has a way of making him a little bit older. Blood pressure goes up a little. This goes wrong and that goes wrong. You look good on the outside. Let's see if you look as good on the inside. At this point, all we need is medical underwriting. Why don't we find out whether or not you qualify?

Then:

> Surely, you can't object to an examination that will cost you nothing, and that will not obligate you in any way. Let the doctor check you up, and let me see if I can get it for you. The company may not be willing to take you. Let's find out first. . . .

Ben comments: "The interview succeeds or fails on my ability to get my man examined. Regardless of what a man says against life insurance, if I can get him examined, I have found that seven times out of ten, he will take it. Get him examined, and it's three-quarters sold. I can also promise you this: if you don't get him examined, you'll *never* get it sold."

Ben often concludes the interview with:

> So, Mr. Prospect, you have a problem. We can do something about it if you qualify. Basically, I have all the information. Give me a couple of weeks time and I'll have something put together for you to see. Then we'll know whether we have something or we don't. Let's find out.

And seven times out of ten, it's a sale.

Ben's Method? It's simply this: "Pinpoint the problem. Offer the solution. Get him examined!"

Follow Ben as he applies his Method to a variety of problems, finds the solutions, and makes the sales. The sales that continue to shatter every existing record. . . .

Part III
Solving the Problems

THE PROBLEM OF THE SHRINKING ESTATE 9

'Let me show you what part of your estate isn't yours....'

Ben has been prospecting and he's discovered a man, age 50, married, with three children, two in college. His business is worth somewhat more than $400,000. He carries $150,000 of life insurance. He has $50,000 in stocks and bonds. He has a problem.

Watch now how Ben makes the prospect recognize that problem (from the tape of an actual interview) . . .

> Mr. Jones, you were good enough to give me quite a lot of information, and I've been doing a lot of thinking about you since our short visit the other day, and I've tried to put together something realistic. I notice, again, you're getting some

silver up there. You've been running pretty hard now for 30 years....

(The prospect agrees.)

And in spite of the tax structure, you've succeeded in building a beautiful estate.

(The prospect is proud of what he's accumulated.)

But (says Ben softly but deliberately) let me show you how much of that estate isn't yours.

Feldman does this with a powerful sales tool. It's a copy of *The Federal Estate Tax Table*, carefully outlined in color to dramatize "the enormous tax bite Washington is waiting to clamp on a man's lifetime of effort the moment he's dead."

Let me show you what part of your estate isn't yours. And from this point on every additional dollar you put into the estate, part of it will be yours and part of it will be the tax collector's.

With this plain device ("Keep it simple"), Ben has struck at a basic emotion: a man wants to hold on to what he's fought for, a man doesn't want to lose what he's acquired by running so hard for 30 years. ("Pinpoint his loss.")

May I show you what happened to some estates?

Feldman then shows him actual records of prominent men who have died in recent years. They're public information, taken from probate records.

Do you remember these people? One was worth $500,000. Another $750,000. Here's an-

The Problem of the Shrinking Estate

other worth over $1,000,000. These men spent their whole lives building these estates to leave them to their families. But it didn't work out that way.

Look at this one. Would you say this man was successful, an estate of $579,000? The day before he died, his inventory in cash was $17,000. He only owed $539. Shouldn't be any problem there, should there? Shouldn't be. Yet... yet, the day after he died ... he owed $169,000 in taxes ... and his cash was still $17,000.

Take this case. He was a member of the original Federal Reserve Board in Washington. He worked with money all his life, yet the day he died he had everything except money. He had $195. The Tax collector wanted $210,000—in cash! Or look at this man—the day before he died, all the money he owed in the world was $500. The day after he died, he owed over $170,000!

And these cases are not exceptions. Look at the others. The story is the same. Look at these figures—and these are actual cases—men who lived, worked, spent their whole lives building their estates, and look what happened to them.

There was enough value in the estates to pay the taxes but there wasn't any cash. None of them owed much money, but, ironically, none of them *had* much money—in the form of cash. They had all kinds of other assets—brick, steel, land—everything except cash. But the Director of

Solving the Problems

Internal Revenue doesn't want bricks. He only takes cash. The need for cash becomes tremendous, but there is no cash. They had everything except cash. And yet the only thing Uncle Sam wants is cash. He wants it first, and he wants it fast.

Uncle Sam will take all your cash, and if that isn't enough—and 9 times out of 10 it isn't—he will simply liquidate the best part of your estate. So you spend 30 years putting it together—and Uncle Sam will take it apart overnight. Is there any reason why Uncle Sam will treat your estate any differently than he did all the others?

The disturbing question has revealed—painfully, forcefully, compellingly—the man's problem: to preserve what he's accumulated over the years, to protect his estate.

*   *   *   *   *   *

Another case: a well-to-do business man without money—a man whose assets have been converted into property—"bricks, steel, land." This man already has a fair amount of insurance, but wants to protect what he has accumulated.

The basic purpose of life insurance is to create cash—nothing more, nothing less. With a piece of paper . . . a drop of ink . . . and a few pennies—you can create more than most men accumulate in a lifetime.

"You know the difference between a big case and a little case?" Ben often asks his audiences. "It's a man with big problems

The Problem of the Shrinking Estate

compared to a man with little problems. All problems have price tags—some are simply bigger than others. Just measure the price tag. My volume tends to become larger (he's still writing just *three* applications a week and has since 1942)—"because my cases have become larger."

The larger cases frequently focus on the problem of estate shrinkage. The bigger the estate, the heavier it's hit by the tax laws. "Most men who build an estate eventually lose it," Ben comments. "They never really owned it. Just leased it . . . and lost it. They call it taxes."

"An Internal Revenue Man," he adds with a touch of humor, "is writing a book called, 'How we made $1,800,000 off the fellow who wrote a book about making $2,000,000 in the stock market.'" The interview continues:

> The day you walk out the tax collectors walk in. They want money, and furthermore, they have a way of getting it. Either you create cash to absorb the tax impact, or the tax impact may absorb the estate.
>
> Now let's take a look at *your* estate. Let's see what your tax bill will be! You're worth about a half million dollars. Let's break it down. Here's a breakdown of your Federal Estate Tax. Minimum $78,000. And if you don't get full credit for your exemptions that can go up to $115,000. And that's not all. The State of Ohio will want $12,000. So here's your tax summary—$90,000! And if you lose your marital deduction, your tax will cost you $163,000! Payable in cash!

Solving the Problems

> Your basic problem isn't whether or not you'll pay your tax, because Uncle Sam has a way of getting paid, but *how* will you pay it? Have you thought about it?

(What's there to think about? The prospect has $150,000 personal life insurance—and he can easily pay his estate taxes out of that.)

> Yes, you *could* pay it with personal insurance. But let me ask you . . . it's *personal* isn't it? Who did you buy it for? You didn't buy it for the tax collector—you bought it for your family. Let them keep it—they'll need it.

Once more Ben has made a strong appeal: "Would you deprive your family?" he's really asking. Of course, the prospect wouldn't. Personal insurance isn't the answer to the tax collector. Then where is he going to get the money? From corporate cash, the prospect replies:

> Yes, you could pay your tax with your corporate cash. I imagine that if I should ask you right now to write me a corporate check for $90,000, you could. It wouldn't break your company. But—I'll bet it would bend it. You simply can't pull $90,000 out of your company and not hurt it.
>
> *Let me pay your tax.* I'll pay it with discounted dollars. I'll pay your tax with dollars that cost only three cents apiece once a year. My dollars will never cost you a dollar apiece. Your dollars have already cost you—considering our tax structure—about *two* dollars each.

82

The Problem of the Shrinking Estate

The mechanics are very simple. You set up a special account and put in $300 a month. My company sets up a special account and puts $100,000 in it. Should something happen to you tomorrow, next week, next year, we simply trade accounts. You take mine, and I'll take yours . . . and mine will always be worth more than yours.

Why don't you let me pay your tax?

This is his basic solution to the problem of estate shrinkage. It's simple—$100,000 or $10,000,000—the proportions—adjusted for the age—hold. And it works.

"Too often when a man falls apart, his estate falls apart. Not because he did something wrong. He just didn't do anything. That's what's wrong. I try to make it easy for him not to make a mistake.

"Why make it hard? Make it simple. Make it easy. Occasionally, I'll take two checks out of my pocket. One for $300—the monthly premium—and the other for $100,000—the estate tax. I hand him the $100,000 check and ask him to sign it. Naturally, he hesitates. Then I hand him the check for $300. Just sign the little one and I'll sign the big one.

"*You send us a premium, and we send you a promise!*"

THE PROBLEM OF THE CLOSE CORPORATION | 10

'I create cash for taxes, capital, salary continuation'

You're realistic and practical in your thinking, aren't you? You'll probably go right on making money, won't you? And in 10 to 20 years from now, your estate won't be worth $500,000 —it'll probably be worth $1,000,000, possibly more. Now you're a millionaire. Let me show you what happens to millionaires. . . .

Remember this one? A world famous accountant. One percent of his estate was liquid, 66 percent was liquidated. This one? Mr. X—3 percent of his estate was liquid and 75 percent was liquidated.

The bigger you get, the harder they hit you. Uncle Sam (unless he'll treat you differently than anyone else), is going to take part of everything you own. *If an estate is worth building, it's worth keeping.* You know the tax must be paid. It's only a question of with whose money—yours or mine. Why not let me pay it?

To the head of a close corporation, the high costs of dying—including debts and estate taxes—pose a particularly severe problem. He has spent a lifetime plowing nearly everything back into the business, and there'd never be enough surplus available to meet the staggering demands of the Internal Revenue Service. But estate shrinkage is only one of the financial problems a close corporation president faces. Here's how Ben pinpoints another—

May I ask this, Mr. Jones, if you were piling up everything you own in one big pile, everything except your company—everything you own: the shoes you wear, your home, your personal life insurance, everything in this *pile* ... and in that *pile* over there, just your company—which pile would be bigger?

So your company is the biggest part of your estate, isn't it? I presume that you have one of those companies that's growing, expanding—you need more inventory, more space, more equipment, more everything under the sun. So isn't it true that the bulk of what you earn is plowed back in—that you take out just enough

The Problem of the Close Corporation

to live comfortably? And you have to keep on plowing money in to keep it healthy? So as the years go by, you're not accumulating dollars. You accumulate brick, stone, steel, machines, land.

Now that's fine as long as you're around. But, unless you have a lease on life, someday you're not going to be around. Ever stop to think, this is a one-man business—your business will last only as long as you do. And what will your widow do with the business?

Your widow should be left something that will take care of her, not something she will have to take care of. She'll want to sell it. You spend a lifetime locking it up, and she'll have to unlock it. How does she plan on getting your money out? It won't be easy.

The moment you walk out, Uncle Sam walks in. There's never any question that she will be able to pay the tax, but since everybody knows she *must* pay the tax and promptly, she must raise cash *fast*. It won't be possible to get a good price on anything she *has* to sell.

If you were going to buy somebody else's company, Mr. Jones, wouldn't you look for a bargain? Others will look for bargains, too, and your company may be one of them. Mr. Jones, would you be willing to sell your company for 25 cents on the dollar?

He would *not*. He's appalled at the idea. He's not going to let a lifetime of hard work and know-how go down the drain. He's not going to see everything he's labored for go on the block for a mere fraction of its value.

All right, Mr. Jones, let's do this. You can keep your company as long as you live, but the day you die, I'll walk in, and I'll buy for cash —you set your own price, set it now, and we'll guarantee to pay it—exactly what you want. At the price you set now, I'll create a guaranteed market for your company.

Once more, Ben has taken a complex financial problem and resolved it in simple terms.

"The biggest problem in a close corporation is simply the fact that it is closed. There's very little market for this kind of corporation, particularly if it is, as most are, a one-man business. The owner spends a lifetime plowing profits back in. But how does he plan on getting them back out? How does someone unlock the cash after his death—and get out the *true* cash value, not the low forced-liquidation value?" Let Ben tell you how another more complicated case was worked out:

"I had an idea. The idea was to lock two companies together. It can be a very simple package, particularly when you find two competing companies in similar fields—the Jones Company and the Smith Company, and you know that either company could operate the other.

"So the Jones Company purchases a half-million-dollar policy on Mr. Smith, and the Smith Company purchases a half-million-dollar policy on Mr. Jones. Mr. Smith and Mr. Jones didn't have the money to pay the premiums personally, so the companies paid it. You know how I sold it?

The Problem of the Close Corporation

" 'Mr. Jones,' I asked, 'would you be willing to sell your company for 25 cents on the dollar?' He was indignant. Of course, he said, 'No!' I then asked him if he would like to buy Mr. Smith's company for 25 cents on the dollar—and, of course, he was quite interested. The same disturbing questions were equally motivating to Mr. Smith. So what we did was lock the companies together. Unusual maybe, but it was just that simple.

"In the event of Mr. Jones' death, a check for $500,000 would go to the Smith company. By agreement they could use it to buy The Jones Company. Mr. Jones' widow would be receiving the agreed value of her husband's company. In the event of Mr. Smith's death, the plan would work the other way around. In either case, life insurance had guaranteed a fair market for either man's company. But it had done more—

"One of the men said to me; 'Well, Ben, I don't know whether I want his company. I'd like to have him buy my company if I die, but I'm not so sure I'd want to have his!' So I said to him: 'All right, so you're going to pay $500,000 for his company, but you're not going to pay much for the $500,000. You'll be buying his company for pennies on a dollar.'

"And in this plan, we were using Whole Life and using a part of the dividend to buy term insurance equal to the increasing cash value in addition to paying the face of the policy. Each man was buying the other's company not for the purchase price of a half a million dollars, but simply with the net cost of half a million dollars of life insurance. And, with a policy that pays the face value plus the cash value at death, the net cost dips down to almost zero. Further, when the Smith company buys the Jones' company, Mr. Smith recovers the block of insurance on his own life—or vice versa."

Solving the Problems

This is a comparatively simple package by which all parties involved benefitted—a package which has succeeded because it is the *only* way of solving the "forced low-value liquidation problem" of a close corporation that must liquidate.

Ben tells of another example of the sales-resistance-breaking appeal of the "guaranteed-market."

"My prospect had absolutely no interest in discussing insurance. He had an estate of about $1,000,000 including $100,000 in life insurance, and about $200,000 in securities and cash. I found out that the cash was pledged to support loans, and that debts would pretty much absorb all liquid assets. The widow would be left with a number of small corporations that she would know nothing about, which she'd be forced to liquidate at far less than their true value. 'How would your wife get any money out of the business if you don't come back tomorrow?' I asked, 'And how would you like somebody waiting with cash ready to buy it at your price the day you walk out?'

"I found a brother, already in the business, quite capable of carrying on, but not capable of buying in. So I created a market. Life insurance was the answer on the split-dollar premium. The cost to the older brother for his portion of the premium was much less than the liquidation cost had he done nothing. To date, I have written $100,000 on the younger brother as part of the buy-and-sell agreement. And on the principal—the older brother—I have placed $850,000. And he was the one who had absolutely no interest in more life insurance!"

* * * * * *

Now listen to Ben as he pinpoints still another problem of the close corporation.

The Problem of the Close Corporation

Mr. Harrington, from what you tell me, I think the bulk of your estate is wrapped up in your company, is that right? (It is.) I believe that you're not paying too much in the way of dividends—that you and your family are pretty much living on your salary? (That's true.) You know that when a man dies, his family goes right on living? And to live they will still need income? Where's that income to come from?

The stock in the company, you say? Sure, they still own the stock, but from an income standpoint it's worth very little. Actually, it creates a need for cash for tax purposes, and yet creates no cash to fill that need. Stock could become a liability, not an asset. [This is especially true when the corporate head holds only a minority of the stock.] The stock in the company is no answer to income needs.

Where do you think they'll look for income? The only place they can—where it's always been coming from—your company. My plan makes this income possible—with no load on your company.

Your family would receive about $200 a week—$10,000 a year—for 10 years—a total of $100,000. Your company would receive $60,000. And the cost? Nothing! Look, the odds are nothing will happen to you in the next 20 years. And if nothing happens, it has cost nothing. Your deposits in 20 years—and the policy value in 20 years . . . look, they wash out!

Solving the Problems

And just compare the cost of paying dividends on stock as a means of providing income with a salary continuation plan like mine. Every dollar the company pays out in dividends costs two dollars. Every dollar paid in salary continuation costs 50 cents. And we guarantee these dollars for pennies apiece!

*　　*　　*　　*　　*　　*

There is a related problem that Ben often tackles at this point. It's the problem of retirement for the head of a close corporation.

As the years go by, you will probably keep on doing exactly what you've been doing ... making money, but plowing it right back into your company, won't you? And it's possible that 20 years from now, you may want to take it a bit easier—maybe you'll have to—the years do have a way of making us a little bit older, don't they?

The same plan that will take care of your tax and take care of your family will also take care of you. It makes it possible for your company to pay you $1,000 per month ... and with no load on your company. Here's how it works—

My company will send your company a check each month for $500 for about ten years—and the check is almost entirely tax free. Your company can then send you a monthly check for

The Problem of the Close Corporation

$1,000—tax deductible dollars. It's a complete wash!

* * * * * *

"You can see the biggest problem in America with closely-held corporations is that they are *closed*. That a man runs and runs and runs. And he makes money and he keeps plowing it back in the company. And it grows and it grows and it grows—and because no man has a lease on life, some day he walks out and a lot of things happen.

"I try to show a man what happens. I try to show that after he has spent a lifetime of effort to build his business, there is still no assurance that what he spent a lifetime putting together won't fall apart over night. Since the tax impact tends to destroy, I attempt to create cash in substantial amounts for taxes, for capital, for salary continuation. I try to build continuity for a man's plans—for his company, for his family."

Does Ben succeed? Of his fabulous sales, the majority come from small, closely-held family or one-man corporations.

THE PROBLEM OF THE KEYMAN | 11

'If a man needs time, he needs life insurance.'

Ben Feldman, as he demonstrated with his "guaranteed market," is a *creative* salesman. He doesn't, as so many salesmen seem to do, accept a standard *product*, and then try to sell it. He finds a need, then *creates* an idea to fill that need. His creations, his "ideas," are put into effect using regular policies, usually Whole Life, or if necessary an option on Whole Life (Term).

For example, the people whose cases are described in the preceding chapters had no need for life insurance itself. They just needed money—payable precisely when needed. So he doesn't sell life insurance.

Solving the Problems

He sells a half-million dollar package designed to create a "guaranteed market" for a close corporation. He sells a million-dollar package designed to convert bricks and steel back into dollars. Life insurance? No! Salary continuation? Yes! Credit floor? Yes! Stock redemption? Yes! Tax impact? Yes!

It is the answers to these big price-tag problems—money problems—that provide the keys to Ben's sales. He turns the keys with the irresistible attraction of life insurance's "discounted" dollars. What are "discounted" dollars? Ben supplies the answer dramatically. At the beginning of a first interview he may flip open his briefcase. Against a red background, an actual thousand-dollar bill stands out vividly.

"I'm selling these in packages of one hundred," Ben says, "How many will you need? The costs?" He points to three pennies mounted by the bill. "Three cents per dollar . . ."

For three (or two, or four) cents on the dollar, (as determined by the prospect's age) the man of means can buy enough to enable his heirs to settle with the tax collector—and leave his other assets intact. Ben's simple packages—built along these lines—provide enough cash *when* it's needed and at the easiest and lowest possible terms. And Ben puts these packages together often enough to create the greatest sales record ever made in the life insurance business.

* * * * * *

What's he selling now? Life insurance? No. He's selling discounted dollars to turn these seven-figure keys:

The key: a package to provide for stock redemption without destroying the company. *Price Tag:* $4,000,000.

The Problem of the Keyman

The key: a package to permit either brother to retain his holdings so that families would have equal share in the business. *Price tag:* $2,000,000.

The key: a package to create a market for minority stockholders in the interests of family harmony. *Price tag:* $1,000,000.

The key: a package to keep all stockholders equal by creating enough cash outside the estate to prevent sale of stock to pay estate tax. *Price tag:* $1,600,000.

The key: a package to put a floor beneath the expanding credit base of a one-man company. *Price tag:* $1,500,000.

The key: a package to provide enforced savings: because some people to save money have to hide it, even from themselves. *Price tag:* $1,000,000.

The key: a package to create an option on tomorrow to offset the company growth. *Price tag:* $8,000,000.

*****

The key: the keyman!

"What's a *keyman?* He's a man whose talents, abilities, experience, and specialized knowledge make him a money-making machine. With him, the company's profit graph zooms upward steadily; without him, the company would suffer an incalculable loss. He may be the boss."

"Why do I need life insurance?" this steel broker countered Ben's overtures. "I own $200,000 now. I've got a million dollars *in cash.* The interest alone will take care of my family. Why do I need insurance?"

Solving the Problems

Because you're a money-making machine. With you here, you can make a tremendous amount of money. You're the money-making machine. You're at work. But with you gone, it'll only be *money* at work. With you here, it's *you* at work ... with you gone, it's *money* at work.

You know the difference? Money at work—what does money at work earn? ... 5 ... 6 ... 7 ... percent? That's about all. How much do the man *and* the money earn? Five times that much!

"Tell me," Ben asks, "is there any man who doesn't want another dollar? I don't care how many he's got. Don't *you* want another one? That steel broker was no exception. Here was a man with nothing but dollars—*and he wanted another one*. He could see that otherwise there could be a loss. The price tag? We discounted future premiums with that $200,000 and then I wrote $500,000 more—and we paid that up. And then I wrote $1,000,000 more.

"But often the keyman isn't the boss. Then it's harder for the man who must say 'yes' to see the need for life insurance. Some big men in the business world just don't seem to understand how life insurance fits in—how a company to grow must keep moving and how continuity depends on key people ... how credit depends on key people."

Ben attempts to explain this with the incisive clarity of his interview technique: a succession of power-packed sales arguments to prove to even the most stubborn man that he does have a problem, and here is the solution to that problem.

As you read the highlights of the interview that follows—and compare them with the earlier interviews you've read (estate

The Problem of the Keyman

taxes, guaranteed markets, salary continuity)—you'll realize that while Ben may have no verbatim sales talk, and while he can easily *ad-lib* to suit the attitude and reactions of each prospect, his interviews do, nevertheless, follow an organized pattern: the presentation of the problem, the goals to make the man anxious to do something about it, the lure of discounted dollars, and the solution in a package that is very easy to understand.

The interview is shown, in the interests of rapid comprehension, on a step-by-step basis. Actually, it's not on the "dotted firing line." There is a progression—a definite logical and emotional build-up from the pin-pointing of the problem to the solution—but it's *not* step-by-step.

Ben may hit a point, move away from it, come back to it circle around it, approach it from another angle, hit again, go off on another aspect of the problem and he is constantly repeating, rephrasing and reshuffling his facts. He is keenly aware that an interview is an interplay of minds, a verbal game for two. When the ball is tossed to him, he must return it: what he says depends on what is said to him.

He is not a lecturer, in absolute control of the audience, able to tick off points, 1—2—3! He is a warm human being, sensitive to the brain and heart of the man he's trying to help. And, above all things, he is responsive to that prospect's immediate thinking. The interview is not a dramatic monologue. It's a conversation. But it's a conversation that—no matter how it may meander or what tangents it may take—always comes back to the original purpose of their meeting. It comes back because Ben consciously *leads* it back!

In the following capsule version of the early stages of an interview, you will observe just one example of how he'll make a point, let its shock effect settle in, move away from it, then return

Solving the Problems

to it with its power to influence greatly enhanced. He may open with—

Mr. Field, how would you like to insure one year's profits? You know, it's almost impossible, Mr. Field, not to make a mistake somewhere along the way. Isn't that true?

Keymen make little mistakes, and a company can absorb little mistakes. But not the big ones. A big mistake could absorb the company. A big mistake is not protecting your company against the loss of a keyman.

Why? You insure your machines. But keymen are machines—money-making machines. Your auditor even puts a box of stationery on your balance sheet, but ignores the man who makes your company a million dollars. While no man is indispensable, neither is your equipment nor your building, and yet it's all insured. Could you get a loan without insuring it? The banks feel the same way about your keymen. Call your banker: ask him if the bank would continue your credit line if he knew your keymen were gone. The day your keymen walk out, the lenders want out.

But keyman insurance does far more than provide a credit base for the company. It creates the cash the company would lose with the death of a keyman. Compare the earnings on money with the earnings on a keyman. One hundred thousand dollars will earn $6,000 interest a year. The same amount wrapped up in a company in the form of a keyman may earn $20,000 to $50,000 or more. The value of a keyman is worth five or ten times the value of money. But your keyman doesn't have a lease on life, does he, Mr. Fields? Some day, he's going to walk out. And then—

What's your keyman supposed to do? Make money. Right? Put me on your payroll, and I'll make as much money and more than any keyman you've got in your company. Furthermore, I'll make it at a tremendous discount. The day he walks out, I'll walk in with dollars—one hundred thousand tax-free dollars. We'll insure him *for one year's profits!*

You can capitalize on the value of your keymen for approximately 3% annually. The cost is offset through accumulating cash value—tax-free—pure profit!

So let's make a deal. My company sets up a special account and puts $100,000 in it. Your company sets up a special account and puts $250 a month in it. It would take a long time for your company to put in the amount we would have to pay out! It takes a long time to pay a dollar for a dollar when you deposit only three cents per year. Then someday, we simply trade accounts.

In business insurance sales, unless you are very careful, the details have a tendency to become overly complex. Ben's packages are very simple and his single-page written proposals follow the same pattern. They're labelled so the single point that he's trying to make is crystal clear—"Special policy for you designed to pay the tax on your estate" or "Designed to guarantee a market for your company" or "Designed to guarantee continuity for your company"—or whatever it is designed to do.

Again and again, it's this ability to reduce insurance to its simplest possible terms that helps create his biggest cases.

The success of Ben's high-price-tag keyman insurance packages is underpinned by his fundamental concept of service. He knows he is performing an indispensable service for all the people who depend on the keyman and on his company. He knows that a man is mortal but a company can be immortal. He knows a company always needs more time to grow, prosper, work out its plans and that a man never dies at the right time.

Ben knows that if a man needs time, he needs life insurance.

THE PROBLEM OF KEEPING A BUSINESS GOING | 12

'Could you run it without money?'

Tell me, what's the most valuable thing you've got?

My company.

Do you want it to continue? Could you run it without money?

Each business insurance case possesses its own key, but the passkey that unlocks all business insurance cases is money. Ben never sells life insurance to his million-dollar prospects, he sells packages—of money. Money, moreover, that can be bought with discounted dollars. And his guarantees mean substantial sums of money will be delivered at some future date exactly when needed.

Seen in these terms, selling business insurance—which may seem complex and intricate to so many—becomes simple. Ben recognizes that his problem as an agent is to find his *prospect's* money problems. Those are the keys, no matter what shape they take. What are these money problems?

"Many money problems center around estate and other taxes. Our tax structure is so destructive, it becomes a major problem for most men to create an estate to take care of those people who are depending on them. If a man does, finally, in spite of taxes, succeed in creating an estate of some consequence, he has an even bigger problem trying to keep it. What do we do? First, we help a man create, then we help him conserve his lifetime of effort. We put foundations beneath men's plans. . . . The tax structure is a tremendous selling tool. Really learn it and you'll sell more."

Growing out of this need for money to pay death taxes come the specific problems of estate shrinkage, forced *versus* orderly liquidation, the guaranteed market. Closely related are the problems of salary continuation and keymen, particularly when that keyman is the same man who runs the company. Listen:

> Could you run your company without money? The day you walk out—Uncle Sam will walk in. Tell me, could you write a check for one-third of your company's value right now? Maybe you could. Maybe it won't break your company, but it will certainly bend it. Uncle Sam is going to take your money. Tell me, could you

The Problem of Keeping a Business Going

run your company without money? *Could your son?*

("But I do have insurance and it's keyman insurance," says the prospect, disturbed but on the defensive.)

I know you have insurance. But when it comes to settling an estate, women and children do *not* come first. The creditors do. Which part of the company is insured. *Your* part . . . or the bank's part? The bank is bailed out, your family is *bought out*. There is no business for the son to carry on. Your boy *can* start over, but why must you compel him to do so?

There are a number of solutions to this problem—a number of ways out of the tax trap—and to provide the son with a cash cushion so he can absorb the small mistakes he's bound to make on the way up. But the core of the problem is to keep the company alive after the death of the father. Then the problem is to prevent liquidation. And the answer, of course, is enough timely cash to pay off the taxes and debts and still leave the assets of the company virtually intact. Here again, the "discounted dollar" answer—

We have a plan that will guarantee continuity of your company until your son is ready to take over. With this plan, you set aside $300 a month. We'll set up $100,000. If nothing happens, eventually we will give you back your money. If something happens, we will give back *your* money—and $100,000 besides.

* * * * * *

"Business continuation can be a particularly severe problem in a partnership or a close corporation operated by two keymen. They are like two men on a see-saw. They balance, but if one man gets off, the other man falls off. It's my job to keep the other man on—with 'see-saw' insurance. I may disturb him by asking:

> How would you like to do all the work and yet share the profits? Yet that's exactly what will happen if you can't afford to buy out his share. If your partner died, what salary would you continue to pay his widow?
>
> And it's best to use life insurance money. Because—while you will be paying $200,000 for your partner's share, you pay very little for that $200,000!

What emerges, as you watch Ben pinpoint and resolve one business insurance problem after another, is the extreme simplicity with which he recognizes and deals with a problem.

"A man can live on credit. But when he dies, someone needs cash. It may be the death of his keyman, or a partner, or a co-stockholder. Then it takes money to assure business continuity and prevent liquidation.

"Many companies are tied down by long-term leases. On buildings. On property. On heavy machinery. The leases might last 10, 50 even 99 years. The dollar liability can be enormous. Imagine a business hit by estate taxes and lease liability simultaneously. It could be devastating. . . . So *another* need for money. You find the money for the prospect in a package designed to underwrite his lease obligation. You ask him: 'Mr. Adams, how would you like to insure your lease liability?'

THE PROBLEM OF KEEPING A BUSINESS GOING

"Let me tell you about the twins. These two boys are in their mid-thirties, and they have a freight hauling company—a lot of heavy equipment. They started out with ten trucks and both of them drove. They worked hard and gradually got to the point where they no longer drove the trucks. Other people drove for them. They were growing. So I called on them. They threw me out.

"Why? They didn't have any extra money. And they were young. They couldn't visualize dying. Not now. Maybe thirty years from now. But not now. So they didn't have any use for me or what I was talking about. They didn't understand it and they weren't about to listen, either!

"But they were growing. And you know what they needed? *Not life insurance—but what life insurance could do for them.* You know what it would do for them? It would help them do what they wanted to do. They wanted to grow. Tell me, how do you grow? You borrow money!

"And when a lender loans you money, you know what he's asking? 'Are you going to pay it back? How do I *know* you're going to pay it back? If you're here long enough you're going to pay it back. Sure! *But do you have a lease on life?* Can you guarantee that you can be here long enough?'

"You know what they needed? They had to put 'certainty of repayment' in their promise to pay. Life insurance *could* do that for them *today*. It will help them get money *today*— money to grow on! Life insurance is a fabulous instrument. So I went down and told them so. And I began to disturb them. I said—

> Put me on your payroll. What do you pay for a good clerk—$85 a week? Will you hire

me? I'll work for $20 a week. What will I do? Something you find it very hard to do—I'll accumulate *cash!* For whom? For you. Hire me, so that the next time you need some money, you don't have to go down to the banker to lend you some. How much? It depends on when you hire me.

It's as though my company set up a special escrow account and put in $50,000. As you pay premiums, money simply piles up. A business should be something to take money out of as well as put into. So I'll accumulate the cash for you— for only $20 a week.

But beyond accumulating cash for you I'll do something else. The day you walk out, I'll walk in—and put $50,000 in the cash register *tax-free*. In your tax bracket, you would have to *make* over $100,000 to equal that . . . probably have to do a million dollars in sales to duplicate it.

Tell me, if you had another $20 in your check book, I don't think you would feel very wealthy. If you had $20 less, I doubt if you'd feel you were broke. Frankly, if you ever get to the point where $20 makes that much difference, you're broke and you don't know it. Put me on your payroll. . . .

"Finally, they did. They agreed to buy term insurance— $150,000 on each. That meant $75 a month apiece. So I 'went on their payroll' for $150 a month . . . And they *did* grow. Today they still have me on their payroll but now I'm getting $2,500 a month . . . on two $1,000,000 policies.

The Problem of Keeping a Business Going

"Sometimes to do what you want to do today, you have to underwrite a bit of tomorrow. Let me tell you about my favorite case:

"He is a real estate developer. Know how much insurance he had in 1946? He had $1,000 with one company . . . $1,000 with another . . . and he didn't want any more. And he wouldn't see me. But he was a builder. And you know where I'd find him? On the job. It got to a point where he'd see me coming—and run the other way.

"But you know what happened in this case? He didn't want life insurance. He could work his money hard, he told me, and make a lot of money. He didn't want life insurance. But you know what? He found out something. He was getting into new projects 'very thin'—and he found out the lenders were a little bit interested in tomorrow. If he had enough tomorrows, everything would work out wonderfully. But if he didn't . . .

"It wasn't life insurance he wanted. It was a *credit base*. So gradually we started putting a cash floor beneath his tomorrows. This made it possible for him to do what he *wanted to do—today!* With the guarantees of that fantastic financial tool called life insurance, he prospered. When I first met him, he had $2,000 insurance. Today, he owns $16,000,000 and it's not adequate because he has a $25,000,000 problem. And I haven't yet been able to get enough insurance to solve it!"

* * * * * *

Ben completely understands the need of a businessman for money today and his need for it tomorrow. Guaranteeing one, he has often solved the other—regardless of the amount of the price tag.

109

THE PROBLEM OF INSURING THE UNINSURABLES | 13

'Borrow someone else's life'

Since money is what he is selling, and not life insurance, Ben even sells *un*insurables.

> All right now, I know you're not insurable, so I'm not going to sell you insurance. I'm going to sell you some money. (You're going to sell me *what?*) I'm going to sell you some money. You're going to need some money. Why are you going to need some money? Because you're a wealthy man.

How's that for an attention-getter? It has everything that a skillful script writer might use: shock, surprise, mystery,

Solving the Problems

suspense—*plus* an implied but profound appeal to the man's self-interest, *and* that magic buy-word—*money*. The old-fashioned peddler prototype may at times have "put his foot in the door," but Ben—in his quiet, modest way—blasts open a sealed door of the mind. Once he has opened it, no one ever closes it on him again.

Listen as he follows up his initial advantage with a variation of his opener. Note that Ben seldom says the same thing exactly the same way twice. His ability to rephrase, paraphrase, state and restate his basic themes gives these presentations a genuine spontaneity.

His interviews never seem stale, never weary. They sparkle. Some of that excitement is an outward display of his deep inner conviction that once again, on each case, he's performing a "very worthwhile service," for his client. But much comes from the freshness of expression—as if he were thinking it out on the spot. His words radiate with the enthusiasm of discovering the way to solve this prospect's particular problem:

> If I recall correctly, Mr. Adams, you say your income exceeds $100,000 a year? (That's right.) Then I assume you have a partner. (A partner?) "Uncle Sam." (Oh, yes.) And he takes a pretty good chunk of that income, doesn't he? (Indeed he does!) Do you find you have much money left over that you can, let's say, put away, save—or does it take pretty much everything to pay the tax and just live nicely? (That's just about right, Ben.)
>
> So you see, you don't really have any dollars. The way you become wealthy—do you

The Problem of Insuring the Uninsurables

know how you became wealthy? You have had your money working very hard. You don't have it in the bank. You've got it in bricks. You've got it in land. You've got it in machines. You've locked it up. You're a wealthy man *but*, you have no money.

Why run hard for 30 years if the net result is 15 years going down the drain? But if the dollar goes through the estate tax wringer, the dollar may go down to 70 cents . . . maybe even 60 cents. Estates fall apart and not because a man did something wrong. He didn't do anything. He didn't do anything and that's what's wrong.

"But *how can* Mr. Adams do anything?" says Ben. "He's *un*insurable, completely *un*insurable! He's waited too long, and he's fallen apart—it's too late! He should not—he *cannot*—buy life insurance—he cannot buy discounted dollars!"

Life insurance is the answer, but since you can't insure *your* own life, we can borrow someone else's life. You need money, and I was going to create some so as to conserve your estate. But you're uninsurable and I can't do that. But there's something else I *can* do. I can begin to eliminate the loss. I can begin to eliminate the loss by gradually moving money from the taxable portion of the estate to where *it's not going to be subject to estate taxes*.

I'll use your right to make gifts: The Federal government levies a tax on your right to make money. They call it income tax. They also tax your right to transfer what's left at your death to your family. They call that estate tax. But the government also gives you a certain right—the right to make transfers free of tax. This is your gift tax exemption. You earn six to eight percent on your money. Some day you'll lose—the tax collector will take—40 to 60 percent, or more. So why not use your tax-free right to transfer to your son rather than the tax collector?

Mr. Adams, do you have any problems—problems running your business? Let me ask you—don't you think that you're the keyman in the operation? Don't you think you're important to it? Do you think you could take one year off without leaving some very real problems? Well, Mr. Adams, someday you're going to walk out—and it's going to be for longer than a year. I've never found a man with a lease on life. Have you?

When you walk out, your boy is going to walk in. He's going to pick up the pieces where you dropped them. And he's going to have problems, too. And they're going to be bigger than yours. Would you like to know why they're going to be bigger than yours? Because you started from scratch. But thanks to *your* hard running, he won't start from scratch! He'll start from maybe $1,000,000 and, you know, his problems will be three times as big as yours.

So why don't we begin at the beginning and give him the advantage of a low, low premium. Would you agree with me that as the years go by the rates go up? Your boy is ten now, and a year from now he'll be eleven—and the year after that he'll be twelve.

Let's do it *now*. Do you think the tax collector will slow down—a year from now, or two years from now, or *ever?* Help him help himself, and you'll do something for your son worth more than money.

You can build something for him that's "out of this world." You can do something for him so wonderful that he'll never forget his father. But you must act now, Mr. Adams: there's a time limit, a legal limit prescribed by government regulations. Annual gift tax exemptions lapse each year on December 31st. Either you use them or you lose them. It costs you nothing to use them. It costs you a lot if you lose them!

"It's not only the son's life that can be borrowed," says Ben. "The wife can protect her husband, too. Or any of the children can do it. Or the entire family. In one case—that of an uninsurable 55-year-old operator of a large truck sales agency—we borrowed the lives of all the other members of the family. We set up large amounts of insurance on their lives designed primarily to utilize maximum rights to make gifts. We could no longer use life insurance to create, so we used it to accumulate. And grandchildren—ah!"

How would you like to take some of the money that would normally go down the drain for taxes and do something so beautiful for your grandchildren that you will never be forgotten?

115

"One uninsurable recently paid up $100,000 on each of seven grandchildren, plus $350,000 for his wife, plus $500,000 and $900,000 for his son and daughter-in-law.

"And so—borrow someone else's life. And do you know something more? Just the fact that the man is not insurable—Wow!—now insurance is tremendous. Now he wants it for *them* because *he* can't get it."

THE PROBLEM OF PAYING THE PREMIUMS | 14

'*Make the tax collector work* for *you....*'

"To buy something a man must have money, and very often your prospect is a well-to-do man without money. Where's the money to come from?

"If you try to make the sale at this point *without* finding the money to pay premiums, you'll be making a fatal mistake. There is no extra money. If you reach into a man's pocket for money, he'll break your arm. Don't back a man into a corner and try to make him say 'Yes.' You see, he's on the defensive. He'll never say 'Yes.'

"Let me repeat: if you're looking for extra money, that's wrong. There isn't any. And not because he isn't *making* money!

Solving the Problems

The funny thing about this man is he makes *more* money than most people. But, first—it isn't all his. Part of it is his, and part of it belongs to the income tax collector. And the part that is left, you know what he does with it? Spends it! He's making more money, so he'd like to live a little bit better. Why not? So instead of two cars, maybe he'll have three or four. I'm not being facetious. I'm only trying to show you why he has no money.

"But I need money, don't I? I can have the best kind of an idea for him—a wonderful thing to do—But there's nothing for nothing! It's not for free! I've got to have money, and part of my job is to find the money. Where? Stop and think. Where might I, logically, first look for money? Now, follow me—

"He's earning money. If I can prevent him from losing some, I've found the money. Now where is his biggest loss? He earns $10,000 a month, but down the drain goes $4,000—maybe more than that. And who gets it? The tax collector. The tax collector is taking almost half his income. He isn't *making* $10,000 a month—he's only *handling* $10,000 a month. It isn't *his*—almost half of it *isn't his*."

If it isn't his money, he should have no objection to spending it. Ben doesn't put his hand in the prospect's pocket. He puts it in the tax collector's pocket—legitimately.

> Why not have the tax collector work for you, instead of *against* you? Money that might otherwise go for taxes can be diverted!

Ben applies the tax regulations as they relate to the appropriate tax-savings device. In his hands, the device—a short-term trust, for example—becomes a powerful selling tool, releasing money for premiums—dollars that otherwise would have gone down the tax drain.

The Problem of Paying the Premiums

* * * * * *

The tax-savings route is one way Ben finds money. Here's another:

"I've been doing quite a lot of this lately. The prospect has a little money—cash—stashed away over here, or here, or over here. You know he's not interested in the return *on* it— only *of* it! But it's exciting to him to hang on to the money. He thinks someday he'll need it, which he probably won't. So I don't have to look for the money. It's there. A block of money.

"I've found the money, but if I put my hand in his pocket. . . . No, I'm not going to ask him to spend the money. I'm simply going to ask him to transfer it. From over here to over here. I'm going to ask him to transfer his cash to a $100,000 policy on his little boy.

"Now why should he do it? I'm going to transfer this block of cash into a paid-up policy—not a single-premium policy —but Whole Life paid-up with discounted premiums. My company estimates, with dividends left to accumulate, that this policy will pay up in 23, 24, or maybe 25 years depending on age." Ben puts it this way to the prospect:

> Getting back to the policy, you know what you need to pay it up? What you're doing is discounting, let's say over a 24-year period. You'll need about $17,000, maybe $18,000, and it's the most amazing thing you ever saw. Here's a $100,000 policy, and as the dividends accumulate, the policy will be paid up. Now where could he put $17,000 and do any more?
>
> And all that boy has to do is leave it alone. It can grow and grow and grow. There's no

investment, no reinvestment. It's the kind of money he isn't apt to lose or throw away, because it takes a little effort to get it. It's an amazing plan.

*   *   *   *   *   *

"Learn the tax structure. It's a tremendous tool. I want my client to use his rights. Uncle Sam clobbers him on income tax, and he's going to clobber him again on estate tax. But Uncle Sam gives him certain rights—the right to make a gift. Why give your money to the tax collector when you can do something wonderful with it for your son? If you don't use it, you lose it. So I'm going to bring him an *additional* policy for his little boy. It will call for a $3,000 annual premium.

"Where's the premium cash to come from? Maybe $2,000 will come just from tax savings, so I can persuade him to give me the other $1,000 a year. You get the feel of this? I'm not going to bring him one policy, I'm going to bring him *two*. I'll bring him one that costs him nothing: it cost him nothing because all we're going to do is move $17,000 from over here to over there. And I'll bring him another one that costs him almost nothing. Maybe I'll bring him *three*. Another $3,000 premium. We'll find the money!

"He'll come up with an annual premium somehow, even if he has to pay it from capital. Remember now, he's a millionaire. He's not running for bread and butter. He's trying to build an estate he hopes to leave for his family.

"Let's help him do what he wants to do. Let's take the money away from where Uncle Sam is going to tear it to pieces and move it over here. In his will, the little boy is to get part of it. Let's put it over there *now*.

The Problem of Paying the Premiums

"So you see, you can take just a simple idea. And you can pyramid it! I had one case sometime back where there were ten—*ten* grandchildren—and we wrote *ten* $6,000 annual premium packages. And it's *good*. Understand it. You're doing something wonderful for the man. It's good."

* * * * * *

And there are other places Ben looks when he's mentally frisking his prospect for cash. Follow this exchange:

> Okay, show me, Ben, where I can come up with the premium money, and I'll—

> Mr. Thorp, I know you've been piling up something over here in stocks. I presume your thinking is you want to have something that will hedge against inflation . . . that will grow. . . . I know you're paying about $4,000 now for premiums a year. Let's take this $40,000 you've got in stocks and use that to pay up the insurance you now have. Then take that $4,000 a year, and you won't have $40,000—you'll have $100,000!"

Ben's plan is simple: He proposes to take the value of the prospect's block of stocks and use that to prepay premiums on his personal insurance in full. Then the money the prospect had been using to pay his personal insurance goes into additional insurance.

> Isn't this a growth investment, Mr. Thorp? Doesn't it grow from $40,000 to $100,000?

> And speaking of growth investments. You know you have to live a long time to prevent

121

Solving the Problems

this from being the best growth investment you ever made. It isn't worth $40,000. It's worth $100,000. And your dividends probably would offset many, many times what you might earn on stocks.

Now, *there's* the money. It's money that you already have. *You* can spend your money, but *we won't spend* your money for you. We'll just transfer it.

Ben has the deep conviction that the life insurance investment is unsurpassed in security, marketability, stability of value, and freedom from care, and has all the other basic qualifications of the ideal investment.

*   *   *   *   *   *

The problem of finding the money to pay the premium is never easy—but usually it can be solved if one knows how to look for it. If the prospect can be kept from putting his hand in his pocket for that extra cash which never seems to be there, so much the better.

As Ben has demonstrated, money can be diverted from taxes; it can be borrowed; it can be transferred from a variety of existing assets. And the client gains substantially. But Ben goes further. Not only does he seem to find money to pay for the premium; he virtually eliminates the premium.

"When I make up an illustration, I often use the Fifth Dividend Option to return the cash value—eliminate the premiums. This way, insurance is free. If that sounds odd to you, take a case and analyze it, you'll see that it works.

The Problem of Paying the Premiums

"Take a man 40 or 45 years of age, and analyze a $100,000 block of Whole Life. You're talking of, roughly, perhaps, a $3,000 annual premium—and it'll generate, a substantial cash value each year. You know, we *must* by contract pay the face value *and* through the "fifth" return the accumulated cash value. But the cash value and the dividends—figure it out yourself, it's simple—they're equal to the premium! They'll think you're crazy. 'It's something for nothing!' But it isn't. It's actuarially and mathematically sound. It's what I call *true* insurance."

THE PROBLEM OF THE YOUNG MAN 15

'I have a special tool designed to create dollars for pennies apiece'

Money doesn't obstruct the sale. Money makes it. For money is the essential reason for life insurance. For the older man, the more affluent, the man in business, life insurance conserves. It shields against tax erosion. For the younger man, life insurance is a miraculous means of creating money instantly where no money existed before.

To Ben Feldman the plan—the policy itself—becomes the bolt of cloth to be fashioned to the shape of each individual's situation. Since it is money that the policies promise, when he fits a package to a problem, he does it—as he expresses it—with "Tailored Dollars." "Tailored Dollars" saves great portions of

Solving the Problems

the estates and businesses of the older man. And "Tailored Dollars" will underwrite the future of the younger man: pay his mortgage, educate his children, build his business . . . and give him that "option on tomorrow."

"Let's talk about a young man. And let's talk about money. Do you know what a young man needs? He needs *time*. Time to accumulate. Maybe he'll have enough time, and maybe he won't. But if he doesn't, life insurance will create what he didn't have time to accumulate.

"Life insurance is time—the time a man might not have. If he needs time, he needs life insurance. Ask him, 'Do you need time?' Disturb him.

"Tell me, who can give him time? The good Lord. No one else. And he's got to have time. I can't give him time. But I can make sure that if he doesn't have the time, his family will go right on living. Don't they have a right to go on living?

"I am disturbing the man, and I want to disturb him, because he's got a problem. And if he doesn't solve it, the problem will still be there, and he'll be transferring it—to whom? His family? They can't solve it either. *He* couldn't. How could *they?* You know what happens? What he should have done, somebody else will have to do. He couldn't. Or *wouldn't*.

"Yes, I'm trying to hurt him because if I don't, he's going to hurt somebody else. He's got a problem. He wouldn't put something first that should have been first. His children's education. His family's security. You know, the years roll by, and nature makes us a bit older.

"Some day a man must die and it's seldom at the right time. In fact, he usually dies at the *wrong* time. He often leaves unfinished business which creates problems. Problems he's leaving

The Problem of the Young Man

his family to solve. Other people to solve for him. Just because he *wouldn't.*

"Why wouldn't he? He didn't protect his family, his future, because he wanted another new car maybe, or whatever it happens to be. Maybe what he wanted was all right—there's nothing wrong with a second car. But it shouldn't have come first. Some things come first. And other things come second. What should come first? I say your family has a right to go on living. *That* comes first."

Decades of successful selling demonstrate that most men will come around to this strong appeal to elemental emotional instinct. Deep-rooted in every man is the instinct to protect his family. But sometimes a fire has to be lit under him to bring these instincts into the open. For the young man, it can be a painful process of self-revelation. He must do something to ease the pain—not just to dull the pangs but make himself feel like a better person. Follow Ben:

> What's the biggest thing you've got? Your life! What's it worth? You put the value on it. Here's how—I'll hire you for exactly what you say you're worth. And I'll pay you right now. All you have to do is work for me for the rest of your life. If you were to die *right now*, you'd be worth the face value of your life insurance. That's the price *you* put on yourself. I didn't. . . .
>
> I have a special tool designed to create discounted dollars—dollars for pennies apiece. Let me show you what I mean —
>
> Give me a nickel. [The young man hands him the coin. And gets back four pennies.] One.

> Two. Three. Four pennies. And I'm going to keep one. Four pennies to one. [He then hands the young man a dollar.] If anything happens to you, you get back your four pennies *and* a dollar.
>
> It sounds like something for nothing, doesn't it? But it isn't. We—the insurance company — use your money. It's simply a tool. A tool designed to create dollars. Dollars for pennies apiece. *When?* When you need it most. And then —*immediately!*

"But he still has to find the money, and that's always a problem. The young man is just getting started—he already needs a million things—and you know what he doesn't have? Money. He just doesn't have any money! He's not kidding me or anyone else. What are we going to do?

"Make it simple. Make it as simple as you can. What can any man need? . . . $100,000 looks like a lot and if you talk about $100,000 he'll think you're crazy. Spread over a 20-year period, this amount won't even give him the $10,000 a year which he thinks his family would need. But there isn't any money, so say to him—

> Larry, this may be what you need, but this isn't what you have. We've got to take something out. What would you like to take out? Let's cut the income down from $800 a month, to $400 a month—to $300 a month.

"Sometimes—you find the money in unusual ways. The prospect may be putting $25 a month into a bank account for his youngster's education. So you say to him:

The Problem of the Young Man

Education for the little boy! Why, he won't go to school for years! But you—*you* might die tomorrow. Put that money each month into this policy!

"What's *an option on tomorrow?* An option on tomorrow quite often is nothing but a block of term insurance, which, for me, 99 times out of a hundred, will convert, and usually on a retroactive basis, at original age.

"Help him by finding the money. When you go back with the policy, try to have found the money. Once you've got it started, you've got the momentum. Once you've got it started, the odds are—he'll keep going.

"Help him by pinpointing the problem. I had a case—a young doctor who wanted to save money. I could have written him a small single premium policy or a high annual premium plan. That would be saving money. His need was to save money, yes. But that wasn't his *first* need.

"He had two little girls for whom someone had to make a home for a good many years. His *first* need was to guarantee income for his family so they could go on living. That was his first need. He wasn't going to retire for a good many years. Saving money for his retirement came second.

"And you know something? Just one year after we wrote the policy he was killed—an automobile accident! Now his family can go on living. Why? Because I pinpointed the problem by establishing a proper order of priorities, then solved the problem with a plan that put first things first.

"A young man needs time to grow on, time to do all the things he's dreaming about. But, you know what else he needs to grow on? Money. There are times when insurance becomes something to grow on. Many times we can take a policy with little or no cash value and borrow money from a bank using it as collateral.

"Some time ago, I wrote a term policy for $1,000,000. He took that million-dollar policy, on which he had paid just six monthly premiums, to a bank—and borrowed a million dollars! There was no other collateral. But the basic problem was that there had to be time enough to complete a program—and my company guaranteed $1,000,000 worth of time. You know, when a banker loans you money, he's interested in just one thing—getting it back. If this man lives long enough he'll pay it back. If he doesn't, we'll pay it back for him.

"There's an old saying: 'Save nickels, and you'll have nickels; save dollars and you'll have dollars.' My phone rang early one morning. A young friend of mine had to have $25,000 fast! I checked his program. He had enough loan value. That night, New York Life mailed him a check for $25,000!

"Let me give you another example of making something fit. He was young—married—had a little boy—making payments on his home . . . and interested in saving about $100 a month. We developed a program, combining low-cost life insurance with disability income protection.

"About a year ago, he was involved in an auto accident—is still totally disabled. All his premiums are being waived and he's getting a tax-free monthly income. That $100 a month he gave the insurance company has already been returned many times over."

* * * * * *

The Problem of the Young Man

The problem of the young man is the problem of creating cash: tailored dollars to meet his very special needs for a *lot more time*. He can buy time with discounted dollars—the time he needs to complete his plans and make his dreams for himself and his family come true. When Ben sells him a simple package, he's simply packaging a dream. It's a commodity for which there's always a seller's market.

TAILORED DOLLARS | 16

'Let me take your problems with me....'

"I really believe in what I am doing—that it is good for you ... and that makes it good for me!"

Feldman makes this credo a living thing by probing into the heart of a man's problem, often revealing it to a man who was completely unaware it existed. Then he solves it—with a simple solution, a fitted solution. He can tailor his dollars to virtually any type of individual, to any type of situation. To a doctor, for example, he'll say—

> You have one big asset—time! So long as you practice medicine, you'll make money. But

death or disability will create problems. Retirement for you is pretty important because you have no retirement unless you build your own! Retirement insurance with waiver of premium in event of disability is a necessity! Why not set aside one office call daily for your retirement?

> The years have a way of making a man old. We have a way of making a man secure. You do a lot of work—you make a lot of calls. Why not set aside just one call each day? You can earn the money; let the life insurance company *save* it for you! You're not smart enough to do both. Look at what it will do for you. . . .

Ben fits his ideas in this same manner to sole proprietors, to rich men, to young men, to partners, to keymen. He likes to use the analogy of the tailor and a bolt of cloth. The bolt of cloth is life insurance, and he's the tailor fitting it to the contours of each individual's needs and capacities. Carry the analogy one step further: in the modern garment industry, custom-tailored suits are often made from general patterns, and these patterns are adjusted to the size and shape and unusual angles of each customer. This eliminates the necessity for basic re-thinking, re-designing of each garment: it boosts production, yet retains that irreplaceable personal element. Here's how Ben might fit a general pattern to one man, the major stockholder in a close corporation:

> The bulk of your income is salary, not dividends. When you die, your salary will stop. How can you protect your widow? How? Sell your personal insurance to your corporation. Take out cash—tax free. Then let your corpora-

tion use the proceeds to set up salary continuation for your widow.

Here are the advantages: No more premiums to pay. You get cash—tax free. You still have insurance through your company. The proceeds still go to your wife through salary continuation.

And another:

You have to be a smart man to make money, but you've got to be a genius to hold on to it! Why not let me pay your tax for you? It's easier to pay it out of income than principal. . . .

And many others:

The law permits you to use corporate dollars to pay your estate taxes instead of personal dollars. So, transfer the estate obligation from personal insurance to corporate insurance. In effect, you can pull out dollars completely tax free to pay your tax. . . .

Section 303 is a tax-free stock redemption designed as a tax relief for a man like you with, say, 75% to 80% of his assets in stock of a close corporation. It permits you to take enough dollars out of the company, income-tax-free, to pay your taxes. We set up the tax money —your executor simply turns in stock certificates to the company and takes retained earnings out tax-free. Money goes in tax-free and comes out tax-free. Where else can you get tax-free dollars today?

Solving the Problems

Look what this does—it relieves you of setting up funds from personal earnings. It releases personal insurance for other purposes. It doesn't tie up large sums of dollars. . . .

Ever stop to think your business will last only as long as you do? Do you have a business continuation plan? It's just good business to own some business insurance. Take three or four or five percent of your average cash balance and transfer it to an insurance account. You will never pay us as much as we will pay you. It could increase the value of your business by 100 percent.

A stockholder's family lives on his salary, not on his stock dividends. There may not be any dividends. And when a stockholder dies, his salary stops. The family may be compelled to sell the stock. So let's guarantee a market for it *now*. Just set aside four percent each year.

If something happened to one of your keymen, you probably would feel obligated to do something for his family? O.K., set up a $50,000 policy. And keyman insurance doesn't cost your company much of anything because it's carried as an asset with a substantial part of the premiums reflected as a credit each year.

Very often the problem requiring a special fitting is the man himself—his health! For the uninsurable, Feldman *borrows someone else's life*. (This is discussed in Chapter 12.) The idea can be fitted to the highly substandard prospect as well.

Tailored Dollars

"There is a different kind of fitting for the man who feels he is uninsurable because of his age—because he has started too late. Two brothers in a roofing company—a growing company. They had spent about 30 years putting everything they had into this company. Actually they took out even less than what they needed to live comfortably. The company seemed to demand all the profits. They also had borrowed considerable amounts of money from banks. One day, I walked in and said:

> Do you know part of this company isn't yours? Look at this Estate Tax table. Unless Uncle Sam treats you differently than he would anyone else, *this* is how much you will owe. Would that be a problem?

"He didn't have to answer. He didn't have any cash! So how was he going to pay out $150,000 some day to the tax collector? But he did have a choice. Or, at least, I thought he had a choice. He agreed to be examined. So did his brother.

"But one man was 59. The other was 61. You see, it's getting late. It may be *too late* when you wait until that time. New York Life rated them pretty heavily. But I finally persuaded them to take two $100,000 policies. Then I asked New York Life to give me $100,000 more on each!

"I went in to see the brothers again and I said to them: 'You know it's late? You're beginning to fall apart. Look—maybe you can run for 10 years more—you can't run for 20 years. Why not *run twice as hard for half as long?*' Now each has two $100,000 policies. They're paying about $2,000 a month for them."

* * * * * *

137

Solving the Problems

Find the problem and the solution, and you've made the sale. Too simple! A man is not a slot-machine: you can't drop in a pat solution and see a sale pop out. A man is a complex creature who, too often, is reluctant to act even when he knows it's for his own good. There's a deep-seated inertia accompanying every decision to part with money. Ben must overcome this inertia. Watch this interplay:

(Ben, before I throw $4,000 or $5,000 a year into this, I'd like to wait awhile, and . . .)

Wait? What would you like to wait for? For the rates to go down? They won't unless you get younger . . . And you know, Mr. Fisk, you could wait *too* long. Mother Nature has a way of making us a little bit older as the years go by. Blood pressure goes up. This goes wrong and that goes wrong. Pretty soon, we don't have a choice. It may be later than you think . . .

(Well, before I do anything, Ben, I'd like to talk this over with my attorney. I'd value his advice on all insurance matters.)

Yes, you have the best advice in the world. Your attorney will do everything he can to minimize taxes now and later. But the only way to eliminate taxes completely is to eliminate the estate completely. And that's a pretty heavy price to pay for your tax.

Your attorney will determine the amount of the tax and minimize it as much as he can. He'll give your widow and your estate all the breaks he can. But when the chips are down—

138

Tailored Dollars

he *doesn't* pay the tax bills—he just figures them out. I can pay them for just pennies on the dollar. . . .

(Ben, I understand everything you say, and I agree. I can get the money. But to do this regularly every year and commit myself in the future—that's a lot of money.)

Let me ask you something, Mr. Fisk, do you plan to live forever?

(No.)

Do you think that you or I have a lease on life?

(Of course not.)

If you can't—if you won't—solve the problem with just pennies . . . well, then, how do you think your family will solve the problem? Problems have price tags—somebody always pays. You've got a problem. Somebody's got to solve it.

You'll have the same problem when I walk out as when I walked in—unless you let me take your problems with me.

And Ben's prospects usually do!

Part IV

Feldmanisms: Ben's Power Phrases and Capsule Comments

The previous chapters provide ample evidence of Ben Feldman's use of power phrases in the course of the sales interview. Concerning these expressions, which have become associated with him over the years, Ben has this to say:

"The expressions, the answers, the statements, and the questions that appear here are not mine . . . but ideas, thoughts, suggestions I have picked up from many, many people over the past three decades. They come from so many men, in fact, that it is impossible to acknowledge my grateful appreciation to each one personally."

But whatever their origin, Ben Feldman has taken these guideline words and transformed them into his own power phrases—his own passwords to success. Reworked and rephrased—and often rethought—they emerge bearing Ben's individual stamp. The vast majority of Feldmanisms transcend the field of life insurance selling; indeed transcend selling itself, dealing as they do with human behavior and universal truths.

FELDMANISMS

Here, then, from his letters, from his proposals, and from the tapes of his talks to many meetings and from numerous visits and personal conversations—is a compilation of the most popular Feldmanisms—the capsule essences of the philosophy and methods that changed a humble farm boy into one of the greatest salesmen the world has ever seen.

One word of caution. Feldmanisms are best understood in relation to Ben's total sales approach. Be sure to read the preceding chapters *first*. Then each Feldmanism will become a springboard for your personalized adaptation of The Feldman Method.

'SECRETS' OF SUCCESS | 17

'My week has seven days'

Feldmanisms

Develop A Positive Attitude

*The biggest asset you have is your earning capacity,
and that depends entirely on your attitude.*

*Attitude is the first and most important factor.
You know that you must sell.
You're not waiting for people to buy.*

*A positive mental attitude—
that, more than anything else, determines your earnings.*

*If you decide you are going to feel wonderful, strong, excited—
then you have the power to move mountains!*

Be Enthusiastic

*The most important person to disturb and get steamed up
in the sales interview is the salesman himself.*

*Enthusiasm is nothing more
than the excitement in your voice.*

'Secrets' of Success

Be Dissatisfied

*Any man who is perfectly satisfied with the way he is living
and the way he is doing his job is in a rut.
If he has no driving urge to be a better person,
or to do a better job,
then he is standing still.
And, as any business man will tell you,
that means the same thing as going backwards.*

*One of man's greatest traits is the total inability
to be completely satisfied with his own handiwork.*

*The feeling of having done a job well is rewarding;
the feeling of having done it perfectly is fatal.*

Feldmanisms

Develop Your Potential

*Make the most of yourself,
for that is all there is of you.*

*Change requires the substituting of new habits for old.
You mold your character and future
by your thoughts and acts.*

*Change can be achieved by changing your environment.
Let go of lower things and reach for higher.*

*The degree to which a man's potential will develop
will depend upon his attitude, his commitment,
his imagination, and his sense of excitement.*

*It's stretching that develops our potential,
And it's excitement that causes us to stretch.*

*When you're tired,
get excited about something.*

'Secrets' of Success

Discipline Yourself

Self discipline comes when you stop doing what you know you shouldn't do, and start doing what you know you should do.

The secret of getting something done is to build a pyramid of priorities. First things come first. Work hard. A twelve hour day is too short. Make every minute count.

My week has seven days.

Believe In Life Insurance

*As an insurance man, you can put foundations beneath men's plans . . .
help make dreams come true . . .
make life worthwhile.*

Make certain it's good for the other man, then it must be good for you.

You make a living from what you get. But you make a life from what you give.

Be singleminded.

Feldmanisms

Know What You're Selling

Be sure,
be absolutely sure,
of what you are doing.

*Lack of appreciation of life insurance
usually stems from lack of understanding.*

*Knowledge makes you strong.
When you really know you know,
you can build a fire under a man.*

*Know what you're talking about, why it fits,
how it fits, the cost of doing something about it,
and the cost of doing nothing.*

*In one word: it's study.
You've got to study.*

*You have to "buy" it first.
Then you can sell it.*

Be sold yourself.

Speak slowly, clearly, softly, definitely, and—be sure.

'Secrets' of Success

Have A Plan

To be successful you must have a plan,
A plan means
(a) goals,
(b) a track to run on,
and (c) a system of priorities—doing first things first.

You must have goals and deadlines—
goals big enough to get excited about,
and deadlines to make you run.
One isn't much good without the other,
but together they can be tremendous.

A track to run on:
Set a quota big enough to get excited about,
then break it into timing, then into ideas,
then into three applications each week.

Would you like to write three million as your goal?
You can't? Too big?
Break it apart into little pieces.
Separate it into months . . . then weeks . . .
then into simple package sales—three a week.
Now it can be done—you have a track to run on.
Make it big enough to be exciting,
then break it down into little pieces so it's do-able.

Organize your time so you put in a full day's work.

Feldmanisms

Think Big

*Don't be afraid to dream big dreams.
They have a way of coming true.*

*Strange as it may seem,
our biggest problem is to sell ourselves.
Most men exchange their lifetime for much too little.
Don't be afraid to think big.*

*Anything your mind can conceive,
that you'll believe, you can achieve!*

*The size of the case will be governed by your thinking.
Think small and the case will be small.
Think big and the case will be big.*

*Begin by building up your own insurance program.
That will raise your sights;
then you can raise your prospect's sights.*

*Why are some cases bigger than others?
Sometimes the only difference is—
little problems and big problems.*

*Think big.
Believe in yourself. Believe in others. Think big.
Don't underestimate your prospect's needs.*

'Secrets' of Success

Prepare With Care

Organize your ideas into a simple sales presentation.

Spend more time in preparation than in presentation.

Never call on a man unless you're prepared.

The sale of life insurance is a procedure, not a problem. It becomes a problem when it stops being a procedure.

Feldmanisms

Prospect With Ideas

*Definition of the best prospect:
A man with a problem—
all kinds of assets, but no money.*

*Prospecting is basically recognizing the problem
and making sure the problem has a price tag.*

Prospecting is simply people plus a good idea.

*Prospect basically with ideas—
ideas designed to merchandise clean-cut,
simple packages.*

*Ask your prospects and clients:
"Would you give me the names of just two people,
successful like yourself,
to whom I might present an idea
designed (for example) to save taxes?"*

*When prospecting, approach the man with a problem
with disturbing questions.*

'Secrets' of Success

Make Calls

One of the keys to selling is simply to make the calls.
Don't make the sales first,
just make the calls and the sales will follow.

Find The Problem

Simply look for the problem, and when you find it,
make sure that you have found it;
that you recognize it; that you understand it so well
that you know the price of doing something about it,
and the price of doing nothing about it.

Pinpoint the problem.
Problems have price tags.

Fit The Solution To The Problem

My work is to make the policies fit.
You know, when you buy a pair of pants or a pair of shoes,
you just don't buy any pair.
You make sure they fit.

Like a tailor with a bolt of cloth,
you must make it fit.

Keep The Solution Simple

*Sell a package—a very simple package
designed to do a special job.
Sell a policy designed to make sure
a wife will never be dependent on her children . . .
a policy designed to convert
bricks and steel back into dollars,
so a family ends up with cash instead of frozen assets.
To repeat, sell very simple packages.*

Merchandise—*simple clean-cut packages,
regardless of size.*

'Secrets' of Success

Don't Sell Life Insurance

Don't sell life insurance. Sell what life insurance can do.
Last year the American people bought 20 million ¼" drills.
Not one of them wanted a drill.
What they really wanted were ¼" holes,
but they had to buy the drills to get the holes.

Your basic purpose is to create money . . .
not to get all wrapped up in something
which is the job
of a trust department, or a lawyer, or an accountant.
Your job is to create not to distribute.

The basic purpose of life insurance is to create cash.
A piece of paper, a drop of ink, and you can create more
than most men can accumulate in a lifetime.

Read and re-read the front page of a policy.

As you solve today's problem,
also try to underwrite a little bit of tomorrow.

Feldmanisms

Sell With Disturbing Questions

*Remember—the key to the sale is the interview,
and the key to the interview is the disturbing question.*

*Use disturbing questions.
—Would you like to insure one year's profits?
—How much time will it take you to pay everything you owe?
—How much is time worth to you?*

Use logic and then emotion.

*There's nothing like a disturbing question
to build a fire under a man.*

Sell Softly

*Don't back a man into a corner and make him make a decision.
Don't push. Lead.
"Let me put something together and you take a look."*

'Secrets' of Success

Get The Prospect Examined

*Regardless of what a man says against life insurance,
if I can get him examined, he's three-quarters sold.*

Stay With Your Case

*Cases grow.
Stay with them, and you will grow with them.*

* * * * * *

*Set a big goal. Make it big enough to be exciting.
Nothing builds a bigger fire under me
than being told I can't do something.
Maybe I can't do it—
but I'm certainly going to try.*

POWER PHRASES AND SALES-TALK IDEAS | 18

'He didn't want life insurance; he wanted what it could do for him'

"Do I use power phrases? I have a book about so thick with power phrases. What they are actually—oh something I heard *you* say, or *you* say—or something I read someplace—and it sticks. I cut it out, maybe rephrase it, put it in the book. Periodically, when you're down in the dumps, when you've been 'thrown out' of the last umpteen places, you read this, and you get, maybe a pre-approach, or a little this, or a little that, or a little something . . .

"But it's not *what* you say that counts so much as *how* you say it. Andy Thomson impressed me early in my career with this important idea: An effective sales approach is important, of course, but it isn't so much *what* you say—it's the *way* you say it—the sincerity in your voice, the way you look at a man. *That* tells him whether you know what you are talking about and whether you are stumbling."

Many of these power phrases and sales provokers appear elsewhere in the book in the context of actual sales talks. They have been arranged for easy reference. First is an alphabetical arrangement by categories. For instance, "Establishing a CREDIT BASE," or "Insuring the KEYMAN." Second is a general section which includes Ben's famous "Put me on your payroll..." in its entirety.

Section I

Power Phrases and Sales-Provokers Arranged Alphabetically by Categories

Creating CASH

*The basic purpose of life insurance is to create cash...
nothing more... and nothing less.
Everything else confuses and complicates.*

*While he didn't want life insurance,
he did want what it could do for him:
create cash.*

*You don't need more life insurance,
but you will need more money.*

*My work is to create cash at a discount
when you need it most.*

*Under our modern plan, your cash value is paid
in addition to the face amount.
Let me show you how it works! (Term Dividend Option)*

Feldmanisms

Protecting The CLOSE CORPORATION

*When a man tries to sell stock in his company,
and people buy it, they buy it
not because of what it is worth now,
but because of what they think he is going to make it worth!
He needs time to complete his plans,
and only we can underwrite time.*

*You spend 30 years building up your company,
and then if you fail to exercise good judgment,
your family may not be able to keep it.*

*The wife should be left something
that will take care of her—
not something she will have to take care of.*

*Your family is suddenly locked into a business
that is not readily saleable, but immediately taxable.*

*One basic problem for the man who has the bulk of everything
wrapped up in a close corporation
is to create cash to absorb the tax.
If he doesn't, the tax may absorb the corporation.*

Providing COMPANY CONTINUITY

*We have a plan that will guarantee continuity for your business
until your son is old enough to take over.*

*Don't saddle your sons with a tremendous tax liability.
Every dollar will cost them over two dollars.
But my dollars cost only nickels
or dimes or quarters, but never dollars!*

Establishing A CREDIT BASE

Putting a floor beneath a credit base simply means underwriting enough tomorrows to pay off what must be paid.

Your banker won't say no when he realizes there is so little difference between premiums going in and cash value piling up.

If you are willing to use corporate credit to borrow a million dollars, then use it to insure the million dollars.

He was a one-man company, and he soon found out that lenders were concerned about what might happen when he was gone.

The policy creates its own credit. The difference between premiums paid in, and cash value piling up is very little compared to the improved company credit.

Power Phrases and Sales-Talk Ideas

Protecting The ESTATE

*It takes a smart man to make money.
But it takes a genius to keep it.*

*Show the prospect an estate tax table, and just say:
"You're about 45, aren't you? Been running pretty hard
for the past 20 years. You've succeeded
in building up a beautiful estate in spite
of the tax structure. Let me show you
what happens to most estates . . ."*

*Some men spend a lifetime
accumulating an estate no larger than this.*

*You know, down through the years, you're continually trading
a day for a dollar . . .
or ten dollars . . . or a hundred dollars
as the case might be.
After 30 years, you have traded your life for your estate.
It represents a lifetime of effort.
Most men end up giving it all back.
They never really owned it—just leased it and lost it.
They call it taxes.*

Uncle Sam has a first mortgage on everything you own.

Feldmanisms

*The day you walk out, the government walks in,
and they want money.
Furthermore, they have a way of getting it.*

*Someday, someone must convert the bricks and steel
back into dollars, because the only thing
Uncle Sam wants is cash.
They have a name for it. They call it liquidation.
That means loss.*

*Uncle Sam will take all your cash, and if that isn't enough
(and nine times out of ten it won't be),
he will simply liquidate the best part of your estate.
So you spend 30 years putting it together,
and Uncle Sam takes it apart overnight.*

*You earn five or six percent on your money,
then the tax impact takes 40 or 50 percent ...
and can very well undo overnight many, many years of savings
and working and effort.
Your estate represents a lifetime ... your lifetime.
If it was worth spending a lifetime to accumulate,
it must be worth keeping.
You didn't build it for the tax collector.*

*Either you create some cash to absorb the tax impact,
or the tax impact will absorb the estate.*

Power Phrases and Sales-Talk Ideas

A man spends his lifetime making money, and, in a case like yours, plowing the bulk of it back into a growing, expanding operation—you never seem to have a great deal of extra cash. Consequently, Uncle Sam wrote a special section of the Internal Revenue Code designed as tax relief for people like you. We designed a special contract that ties in, and creates the cash. Very simple. Your company sets up a special account and puts $10 a day in it. My company sets up a special account and puts $100,000 in it. Some day we simply trade accounts. How long would it take your company at $10 a day to put in enough to pay your estate tax?

It is much easier to pay the tax out of income than out of principal— because principal means liquidation. A man doesn't always die at the right time, and then it could mean forced liquidation.

There are two ways to pay your tax: with your dollars or my dollars. My dollars cost pennies apiece. Your dollars cost two dollars apiece. Why not use mine?

Our tax structure is so realistic that it becomes a major problem to accumulate an estate. And if, in spite of taxes, you do succeed, you have a bigger problem trying to keep it. With a drop of ink, we create an estate and then we conserve it. You send us a premium, and we send you a promise. Together we make dreams come true.

FELDMANISMS

Selling An EDUCATIONAL PACKAGE

Your child may have a "right" to a good education, but it's going to take money to exercise that right.

Getting The MEDICAL EXAMINATIONS

You know, a man pays a price for success. Mother Nature has a way of making us a little bit older as the years go by. Let's see if you look as good on the inside as you do on the outside.

Power Phrases and Sales-Talk Ideas

Utilizing GIFT TAX EXEMPTIONS

The government levies a tax on your right to make money. They call it income tax. The government levies a tax on your right to transfer what's left to your family. They call that estate tax. But, the government also gives you a right—the right to make liberal transfers of property free of tax. We call this your gift tax exemption. Gift tax exemptions lapse each year on December 31st. Either you use them or lose them. Costs you nothing to use them . . . costs you a lot if you don't. Use them or lose them!

How would you like to take some of the money that normally goes for estate taxes and do something for your grandchildren in such a way you will never be forgotten?

This plan will not only reduce your estate tax, but it will set up a substantial estate for your son. The estate for your son is many times the amount of the gift.

Probably the best solution to the premium payment problem where the wife owns the policy is for her husband to make gifts of cash to her, which she then may, if she chooses, use to pay the premiums on her own behalf.

Feldmanisms

Creating A GUARANTEED MARKET

*One of the biggest problems in a close corporation
is the very fact that it is closed. You spend 20 years
plowing money back into the corporation, and then someday
your family has the problem of getting it back out. I have an idea
that will guarantee a market for your company ...
for pretty close to 100 cents on the dollar
—and yet my dollars could cost you only pennies apiece.
You spend a lifetime plowing money in.
There should be some assurance of getting it back out.
Yes, there are two ways of getting it back. One is orderly;
the other forced. And they have a name for it—
they call it liquidation.*

*There was never any question that she could pay the tax.
But, everybody knew she had to pay the tax, and so
it was not possible for her to get a good price on anything
that had to be sold. Let me show you how to
protect your widow against bargain seekers.*

*I will create a guaranteed market ... a policy designed
to convert bricks and steel into dollars
so your family ends up with dollars instead of frozen assets.*

Insuring The KEYMAN

Some of the biggest men in the business world fail to understand life insurance ... that for a company to grow it must keep moving, and that continuity depends on key people.

It's almost impossible not to make a mistake somewhere along the way. The difference is keymen make little mistakes, and a company can absorb little mistakes. But not the big ones—they quite often absorb the company!

Machines don't make money. Only management—keymen—make money. When you lose a keyman you lose money. They should be insured to indemnify the company.

Compare the earnings on money with the earnings of a keyman. One hundred thousand dollars will earn $5,000 a year. The same amount wrapped up in a company operated by a keyman may earn $20,000 to $50,000. The value of a keyman is many times the value of money.

FELDMANISMS

Your keyman is a money-making machine. With him here, there is a man at work. With him gone, it would simply be money at work. The contrast would be tremendous.

Your accountant even puts a box of stationery on your balance sheet, but ignores the man who makes your company a million dollars. While no man is indispensable, neither is your equipment, nor your building—and yet equipment and building are insured . . . because you can't get a loan without it.

When the keyman walks out, the lenders want out.

The ability of keymen means the difference between profit and loss. Insuring your keymen means insuring profits. My company offers a policy that costs four cents per dollar, but returns the dollar plus three cents out of every four.

The keymen are worth what you insure them for . . . and should be insured for what they are worth.

Capitalize on the value of your keyman. It can be done for approximately three percent annually. The cost is covered through accumulating cash value with face value, tax free and pure profit.

Use a special split-dollar policy designed to create a cash cushion for your company.

*If you don't have a keyman worth insuring,
you don't have a keyman.*

*There is no cost for keyman insurance.
Only a cost for not having it.*

Buying the PARTNER'S INTEREST

See-saw insurance is simply two men operating a partnership. One gets off, the other falls off.

A special purchase policy designed to buy a partner's interest: each of you sets up a special account. Each puts in $10 a day. We put $10,000 each in separate accounts. The day your partner walks out, we simply trade accounts— the $10 a day account for $100,000.

With this plan you set aside $300 a month. If nothing happens, we will give you back your money. If something happens, we will give you back your money, and his share besides.

It's better to use insurance because, while you pay $500,000 for your partner's share, you pay very little for the $500,000.

Insuring the PROFESSIONAL MAN

The professional man leaves his family a highly educated brain— not a going business.

FELDMANISMS

Providing For SALARY CONTINUATION

*The bulk of your worth is wrapped up in your company,
isn't that right?
You're not paying much in the way of dividends,
just taking out enough salary to live on comfortably.
Ever stop to think that the day you walk out, your salary stops—
but your family goes on living? They will still need income—
where do you think they will look for it?
Exactly where it's been coming from—your company. So why
don't you make sure your company can do what you will want it
to do, and what it will have to do—
take care of your family?
My plan makes this possible with no load on your company.*

*When a stockholder dies, his salary stops.
His family goes right on living. May I ask you on what?
They still own the stock, but from an income standpoint,
it's worth very little. Frankly, it creates a need for cash
for estate tax purposes, and yet creates no cash.
It could become a liability, not an asset.*

Power Phrases and Sales-Talk Ideas

A man's family should never be dependent on his business after he's gone. Many times it goes downhill a lot faster than it went up. This plan will bail out anyone who walks out, without drowning the survivor.

Just compare the cost to your company of $10,000 a year in dividends with $10,000 a year in salary continuation. Dividend cost is $20,000. Salary continuation is only $5,000.

Compare the cost of paying dividends on stock to provide income with a salary continuation program backed up with keyman insurance. Every dollar the company pays out in dividends costs two dollars. Every dollar paid in salary continuation costs 50 cents. And we guarantee the dollars for pennies apiece.

Preparing For RETIREMENT

*Old age needs so little,
but it needs that little so much.*

*Men think because they're always working with money,
they will always have money.
T'aint so!*

You may last longer than your money.

*The years have a way of making a man old.
We have a way of making him secure.*

*Some men have to hide money—
even from themselves.*

*Doctor, why not set aside just one call each day.
Look what it will do for you...*

Section II

Power Phrases and Sales Provokers In General

You will be worth the most when you're worth the least. The years roll by, and nature makes us a bit older. Someday a man must die, and it's seldom at the right time. In fact, he usually dies at the wrong time. He often leaves unfinished business which creates problems. Regardless of how important a man is while he is here, many things fall apart when he's gone! The plan insures the most precious thing you have—life. Have you ever considered your body and your brain are worthless when you are dead? With this plan, you will become worth the most when you are normally worth the least. Let me show you how it works....

No man dies at the right time.

Good health is yours on a day-to-day basis.

A man needs credit to live, but cash to die.

Feldmanisms

No one ever died with too much money.

*True wealth is money to spend, not money to manage.
We spend income, not principal.*

*Life insurance is simply a partnership: a man and time.
Each day he trades a day for a dollar.
At the end of a lifetime, he has exchanged time—his lifetime—
for property values. We guarantee the time.*

*A debt should last no longer than
the man who created it.*

*The best investment in the world is
the one that pays most when you need it most—life insurance.*

*Whether you buy the policy or not,
somebody in the end will pay for it.*

*Life insurance is time. The time a man might not have.
If he needs time, he needs life insurance.*

*Insurance is the only tool
that takes pennies and guarantees dollars.*

Power Phrases and Sales-Talk Ideas

Problems are price tags. Somebody always pays.

You know why you need money? You're a wealthy man.

Most men have two problems:
first, to accumulate; then, to conserve.

Pay premiums out of capital.
When you can buy dollars for pennies apiece,
you would have to live a long, long time
to keep such a policy from being
the best growth investment you ever made.

Most men don't do anything wrong.
They don't do anything. That's what's wrong.

Feldmanisms

Put Me on Your Payroll

Mr. Brown, what do you pay for a good clerk? Eighty-five dollars a week? I'm looking for a job. Will you hire me? I'll work for $20 a week. What will I do? Something you find it very hard to do—accumulate cash. For whom? For you. Hire me, so the next time you need money, you won't have to go down to the bank and ask the banker to lend you some. How much? It depends on when you hire me.

Statistics show that most men in a growing, expanding business take out only enough money to cover their expenses. Everything else they keep plowing back in. More inventory, more equipment, more everything—except more money for themselves. You know, a business should be something to take money out of as well as to put money in. But, beyond accumulating cash, I will do something else for you. The day you walk out, I'll walk in. I'll put $50,000 tax-free in the cash register. In your corporate tax bracket, you would have to make over $100,000 to equal it—probably have to do $1,000,000 in sales to duplicate it. Tell me, if you had another $20 in your check book, I don't think you would feel wealthy. If you had $20 less, I doubt if you would feel that you were broke. Frankly, if you ever get to the point where $20 makes that much difference, you're broke, and you don't know it.

Power Phrases and Sales-Talk Ideas

The plan is very simple. My company sets up a special account and puts in $50,000. Meanwhile, it's insurance, too. Should something happen to you, instead of the $20 a week you put in, we'll pay the $50,000 we put away. This represents what you intended to put aside over the years.

May I start working for you now? Put me on your payroll!

DISTURBING QUESTIONS | 19

'Did you ever find a man who had a lease on life?'

Protecting the CLOSE CORPORATION

Tell me, what's the biggest thing you've got—your company? Could you run it without money? ... The day you walk out, Uncle Sam will walk in. He'll take all your money.

Yes, I know, you probably could write a check for $200,000, and it wouldn't break your company—but, boy, I'll bet it would bend it. You know there's an easier way of doing it. Why don't you let me pay your taxes?

Would you like to insure your lease liability?

183

Providing COMPANY CONTINUITY

Ever stop to think your business will last only as long as you do?

Tell me, what's the most valuable thing you've got? Your company? Want it to continue? Could your son run it without money?

Your boys can *start over—but why must you* compel *them to do so?*

Establishing a CREDIT BASE

How much time would it take to repay everything you owe? How much is that time worth to you?

Do you think your bank will extend the same credit line to the man who takes your place?

You pay a bank 6 to 8 percent for a debt—why not pay us 3 percent for an asset?

Disturbing Questions

Protecting the ESTATE

Could you, right now, give me one-third of everything you own?

Look, here are authentic cases. Look at this one. Wealthy man while he lived—problems when he died. One percent was liquid and 66 percent was liquidated. Tell me—if you were the executor of this estate, what would you do?

Could you, right now, pay out 30% of everything you own without creating some difficult problems?

Would you say six or seven percent is a fair return on your money? Do you know what Uncle Sam is going to take— 30 ... 40 ... even 50%—and call it taxes?

If your estate was worth building, it's worth keeping— why not try to keep yours?

Why run hard for 30 years, if the net result is 15 years going down the drain?

Why pay tax out of principal?

Either you create some cash to absorb the tax, or the tax may absorb your estate!—Do you realize that?

It isn't a question of if you'll pay the tax; the only question is with whose money—yours or mine?

There are two ways to pay your tax: with your dollars or with my dollars; my dollars cost pennies apiece, your dollar costs two dollars—why not use mine?

Feldmanisms

Utilizing GIFT TAX EXEMPTIONS

You earn four to six percent on your money, and then someday lose 40 to 60 percent, so why not use your tax-free right to transfer to your children rather than transfer to the tax collector?

Creating a GUARANTEED MARKET

What will your wife do with your business? You know, you spend a lifetime plowing money in—shouldn't there be some way of getting it back?

If you were going to buy your competitor's company, and you knew he had to sell, would you pay 100 cents on the dollar or look for a bargain?

Would you sell your interest for pennies on the dollar?

Would you like to create a guaranteed market for your company?

Let me buy your company—how much is it worth?

How would your family get any money out of the business, if you don't come back tomorrow?

How would you like somebody waiting with cash ready to buy at your price the day you walk out?

Tell me, which would you prefer: for your family to remain locked in after you're gone? Or when you walk out, have our money walk in?

Disturbing Questions

Insuring the KEYMAN

Would you like to insure one year's profits?

Why don't you capitalize the value of your keymen? They're going to wear out just like the machines you depend on.

Buying the PARTNER'S INTEREST

How would you like to do all the work, and yet share the profits?

How would you like to buy your partner's interest for pennies on the dollar?

For $50 a week, I'll pay your partner's family $100,000, and return the bulk of the $50 a week—do you know of an easier way to bail out your partner?

Providing for SALARY CONTINUITY

When a stockholder dies, his salary stops, but his family goes on living—may I ask on what?

Want your family to be dependent on your company after you're gone?

If your partner dies, what salary would you continue to pay his widow?

Feldmanisms

Disturbing Questions in General

How much is a man's life worth?

What arrangements have you made after your insurance runs out?

People never die at the right time! What makes you think it will be different for you?

All your life you exercised good judgment—why not do so now?

Why should a lifetime of giving be forgotten?

Do you ever have a problem, or does everything always run smoothly?

How much time do you need to complete your plans?

Did you know out of eight men between the ages of 45 and 54, one of them will run out of time in the next year?

TOOLS FOR MAKING SALES | 20

'You can buy dollars for pennies apiece'

"The purpose of a sales aid," says Ben, "is to get the man's attention. If you give me something to get the man's attention, I'm better able to make the sale.

"The first tool is a blow-up of the Federal Estate tax table... (see page 190)

"... I'll place that before a man and simply say:

> Part of what you own isn't yours. Let me show you the part that isn't yours. And from this point on, every additional dollar you put into the estate, part of it will be yours and part of it will belong to the tax collector.

FELDMANISMS

Federal Estate Tax — Present Rates *

Net Estate (After all deductions and $60,000 exemptions)	THIS PART ISN'T YOURS Total Tax	Block			Rate
$ 0	$ 0	$ 0	to	$ 5,000	3%
5,000	150	5,000	to	10,000	7%
10,000	500	10,000	to	20,000	11%
20,000	1,600	20,000	to	30,000	14%
30,000	3,000	30,000	to	40,000	18%
40,000	4,800	40,000	to	50,000	22%
50,000	7,000	50,000	to	60,000	25%
60,000	9,500	60,000	to	100,000	28%
100,000	20,700	100,000	to	250,000	30%
250,000	65,700	250,000	to	500,000	32%
500,000	145,700	500,000	to	750,000	35%
750,000	233,200	750,000	to	1,000,000	37%
1,000,000	325,700	1,000,000	to	1,250,000	39%
1,250,000	423,200	1,250,000	to	1,500,000	42%
1,500,000	528,200	1,500,000	to	2,000,000	45%
2,000,000	753,200	2,000,000	to	2,500,000	49%
2,500,000	998,200	2,500,000	to	3,000,000	53%
3,000,000	1,263,200	3,000,000	to	3,500,000	56%
3,500,000	1,543,200	3,500,000	to	4,000,000	59%
4,000,000	1,838,200	4,000,000	to	5,000,000	63%
5,000,000	2,468,200	5,000,000	to	6,000,000	67%
6,000,000	3,138,200	6,000,000	to	7,000,000	70%
7,000,000	3,838,200	7,000,000	to	8,000,000	73%
8,000,000	4,568,200	8,000,000	to	10,000,000	76%
10,000,000	6,088,200		All over	$10,000,000	77%

* The exemption is that allowed by the 1942 Revenue Act, while the rates are those imposed under the 1941 Revenue Act, which were NOT changed by the later law. The tax established by the application of this rate schedule is reduced by the credits for state inheritance taxes and prior gift taxes, and the remaining figure is the NET FEDERAL ESTATE.

BF69-1-C

"Now let's look at the Estate of Mr. M. . . .

FREDERICK C. M.

Died March 4, 1961, age 69	SETTLEMENT COSTS	
	Debts	$ 30,767
Gross Estate $935,861	Administration Expense	9,690
	Attorney's Fee	15,000
Total Costs 361,469	Executor's Fee	30,000
	Pennsylvania Inheritance Tax	49,400
Net Estate $574,392	* Federal Estate Tax	226,612
Cash in estate, $11,849	TOTAL COSTS	$361,469
	* No marital deduction; no spouse surviving.	
CASH — $11,849	COSTS — $361,469	

"These are actual probate records, and they're public records so there's nothing wrong with displaying them as they are here. Now, you see the name, who he was, when he died. Mostly, you see the thing that hurts most estates.

> Look at this one. The day before he died, he owed roughly $30,000. This was every dime in the world he owed the day before he died. The day after he died, he owed more than $360,000.

191

"Now let's take a look at the estate of John Doe...

FOR JOHN DOE

TAX IMPACT ON ESTATE OF:	$500,000
1. Federal Tax	$ 50,000
2. State Inheritance Tax	$ 16,000
3. Administration costs (approximately 4%)	$ 20,000
4. Miscellaneous Items (Income Tax accrued, etc.)	$ 5,000
TOTAL	$ 91,000
CASH CUSHION TO COVER PERSONAL COMMITMENTS	$100,000
TOTAL CASH REQUIREMENT	$191,000

WHO WILL PAY THIS?

WHY NOT USE DISCOUNTED TAX-FREE INSURANCE DOLLARS?

"Here's what I'm trying to do: show a man again that part of what he owns isn't his. And, first, we have figures on a half-million dollar estate. It's logical to assume this man will continue doing what he's been doing, making money. Time will go by, the estate will grow—and I'm trying to show him that if he *doesn't* buy *now*, the problem will only become bigger!

"So I move from a half-million on over to the million, and when I write the application I order a policy to cover the tax on the million. You'll be amazed how many times you'll place that larger policy instead of the first one.

FOR JOHN DOE

TAX IMPACT
ON ESTATE OF: ONE MILLION DOLLARS

1. Federal Tax	$110,000
2. State Inheritance Tax	$ 37,000
3. Administration costs (approximately 4%)	$ 40,000
4. Miscellaneous Items (Income Tax accrued, etc.)	$ 20,000
TOTAL	$207,000
CASH CUSHION TO COVER PERSONAL COMMITMENTS	$200,000
TOTAL CASH REQUIREMENT	$407,000

WHO WILL PAY THIS?

WHY NOT USE DISCOUNTED TAX-FREE INSURANCE DOLLARS?

"Now let's look at the special policy for John Doe . . . (See page 194)

Feldmanisms

MILLION DOLLAR POLICY

YR.	ANNUAL PREMIUM	INCREASE IN CASH VALUE	TERM COST	DISCOUNTED DOLLARS FACE VALUE ..plus..	ACCUMULATED CASH VALUE	TOTAL
1969		$ 16,000	$ 48,090		$ 16,000	$1,000,000
1970		$ 38,000	$ 26,090		$ 54,000	$1,000,000
1971		$ 47,390	$ 16,700		$101,390	$1,101,390
1972		$ 47,660	$ 16,430		$149,050	$1,149,050
1973	$ 64,090	$ 47,790	$ 16,300	$1,000,000	$196,840	$1,196,840
1974		$ 41,850	$ 22,240	TAX-FREE	$238,690	$1,238,690
1975		$ 41,680	$ 22,410		$280,370	$1,280,370
1976		$ 40,270	$ 23,820		$320,640	$1,320,640
1977		$ 38,530	$ 25,560		$359,170	$1,359,170
1978		$ 71,136	+ $ 7,046		$430,306	$1,430,306
Total-	$640,900	$430,306	$210,594			
Average-	$ 64,090	$ 43,031	$ 21,059			

(Dividend and interest estimates are based on current illustrations and are not guarantees or promises of future dividend results.)

194

Tools for Making Sales

"This is nothing except a block of Whole Life. And all I've done is accumulate the premiums and the cash values, and show the term cost on an annual basis year by year until I get down to the tenth year. There I show that premiums for ten years amounted to so much . . . cash value at that point was so much—and the difference is very little, a little over $20,000. And for the $20,000 we took out of your company, we're going to put $500,000 back in—tax free!

"And what I'm doing under the head, 'TAX-FREE PROCEEDS,' is showing the face value of $500,000 plus the accumulated cash value as the total amount payable. And if you compare the accumulated cash value with the accumulated premiums, you'll find it's pretty much a return of premiums."

* * * * * *

Ben uses other tools as well. For shock value, a $1,000 bill with three pennies mounted on it is an unparalleled attention-getter. And his check-choice tool—"Hand him two checks. One for $300 and one for $100,000. Ask him to sign one . . ." is a peerless example of a close. But his real tool is something else again, something quite basic. Listen to him use it—

> Mr. Smith, every day you fight to make money. Every day you face decisions. You try to make only the right decisions, not the wrong ones. If anything looks like it will lose you money, you'll shy away from it. You won't touch it with a 40-foot pole. If it looks as though it will make you money, you're interested. We have a tool designed to discount your tax. You can buy dollars for pennies apiece. You know what I do? I sell money. I create cash. *This* is my tool.

ANSWERING OBJECTIONS 21

*'Paying the premium isn't the problem.
Paying the premium is the solution.'*

Why should a man object to something that's unquestionably good for himself, his family, his business, his business associates, his employees? If this reluctance to part with money even for one's own self-interest were not one of the most perverse of all human characteristics, insurance companies wouldn't need salesmen: a single presentation by mail or advertisement would make insurance converts of us all. But this cash-inertia is a fact of life. It takes very definite and repetitive shapes—"the objections." Feldman knows them all. And he knows how to overcome them. Here is a sampling of the most commonly used objections, and the Feldmanisms which turn them into sales. . . .

Feldmanisms

(In selling the man of means or the close-corporation head)
OBJECTION: *I don't have the money.*

Some things come first. Some come second. Your family should have the right to go on living. That should not come second. When it comes to settling an estate, women and children don't come first—your creditors do.

If you can't solve the problem with pennies, how do you think your family can solve it? They will need dollars. Certainly, you have a lot of assets in your company—it's worth over $500,000—but, may I ask you: is that $500,000 in dollars—or is it wrapped up in bricks and steel?

There are all kinds of tools, each designed to do a special job. The tool designed to do a special job will do it better than something you may substitute. What I am talking about is a special tool; it's designed to discount taxes. It produces dollars at four cents!

I'm forever broke. But I'm broke because I'm *saving* money. Quite a contrast between being broke because you're *spending* money.

A man spends his lifetime making money, and in a case like yours, plowing the bulk of it back into a growing, expanding operation. Never seems to have a great deal of cash. But there's a special section of the Internal Revenue code designed as tax relief for you. We designed a special contract that ties in and creates cash—very simply. The company sets up a special account and puts $10 a day into it. My company sets up a special account and puts your estate tax in it. Someday, we simply trade accounts. *How long would it take your company—at $10 a day—to put in enough to pay your estate tax?*

If you think you can afford this insurance, or if you think you *can't*—you are absolutely right ... because the world places the same value on you that you place on yourself.

*　　*　　*　　*　　*　　*

(In selling the close-corporation head)

OBJECTION: *I have sufficient insurance.*

Fine, what you've done is bail out your creditors, but locked in your family.

Which part of the company is insured? Your part or the bank's part? Who gets his money out, and who remains locked in?

*　　*　　*　　*　　*　　*

(In selling anybody)

OBJECTION: *I prefer to buy stocks and a better return on my money.*

Life insurance doesn't offer you spectacular returns on your money, but it guarantees the return of your money.

Feldmanisms

The stock market is where money makes money. Life insurance creates money—where none existed before.

You would have to live a long, long time to keep a policy paid from capital from being the best growth investment that you ever made.

* * * * * *

(In selling the wealthy man or the close-corporation head)

OBJECTION: *I'd like to talk to my attorneys and accountants.*

Fine. That's wonderful. But what do you want to talk about? There isn't anything to talk about until we find out if we can get it. When everything is said and done, you know what the lawyer will do? You know what the auditor will do? They'll do their very best to keep you on the right track and minimize your loss—but when the chips are down, they won't pay bills. They will just figure them out.

I can give you anything you want in the way of a proposal. But, you know, there's no assurance that we can get this. Before you talk it over with your attorney, let's see if we have something to talk about. All that I need now is medical underwriting. Then we'll know. Give me about three weeks time and I'll be back. Then we'll know whether we do have something or we don't have something to present to your attorney.

ANSWERING OBJECTIONS

If your lawyer says you don't need the insurance, then I say, "Fine, but I want it in writing. You have a problem we are willing to solve for pennies on the dollar. If he says no, I'd like his letter in my files."

The only thing I want to do for you is make money. Certainly, your accountant will not object to that.

Did you ever find a lawyer who *paid* the tax—didn't he just figure it?

If you had died yesterday, who would pay what would have to be paid—your lawyer? —your accountant?—or your family? Could your family pay it for $10 per day? Could they even *borrow* the money they would need for $10 per day?

* * * * * *

(In selling anybody, but particularly the wealthy man and the close-corporation head)

OBJECTION: *I'd like to wait.*

You would like to wait? Why?

You would like to wait? For what? For the rates to go down? They won't unless you get younger.

The cost of a life insurance policy increases each year if you *don't* have it, and decreases if you *do* have it!

201

Feldmanisms

I hope your stocks increase four or five percent each year. Because that's the very least you must earn to equal the permanent increase in your insurance premiums by waiting. In addition, you risk your insurability. Net result: you never pay less, you always pay more.

O.K., you're realistic and practical in your thinking, aren't you? And you're making money, and you'll go right on making money, won't you? And ten to twenty years from now, your estate won't be worth $500,000. It will be worth a million—probably more. You will be a millionaire, but let me show you what happens to a millionaire. . . . Remember him? Biggest accounting firm in U.S.! One percent was liquid and 66 percent was liquidated. *The bigger you get, the harder they hit you.* Uncle Sam, unless he treats you differently than everyone else, is going to take part of everything you own. Why wait?

A moment ago, you agreed that no one has a lease on life. It isn't a question of "if" . . . it's a question of "when"—why wait?

You must use your gift tax exemptions before December 31st. Use them or lose them!

Let's compare the cost of buying it with the cost of not buying it . . . There's a price tag on everything. There will be a cost either way—if you do, or if you don't. Compare the cost. Your estate represents your lifetime. Is it worth keeping? *Why wait?*

ANSWERING OBJECTIONS

(In selling the substandard risks)

OBJECTION: *I object to paying extra premiums.*

Better to accept it now, even though by waiting you might qualify for standard insurance. As the years go by, the rates go up. Your rating today might be a temporary increase in premiums, while the increase as the years go by is a permanent increase—payable for the rest of your life.

This premium is the *standard* rate for people with a history of high blood pressure, diabetes (or other medical impairment).

*　　*　　*　　*　　*　　*

(In selling anybody)

OBJECTION: *I have a friend in the business.*

Many men prefer not to discuss personal or business matters with a friend.

*　　*　　*　　*　　*　　*

(In selling the wealthy man)

OBJECTION: *Too much money will spoil my son.*

It isn't too much money, but too little character. But your son, like you, will have character.

*　　*　　*　　*　　*　　*

Feldmanisms

(In selling keyman insurance)

OBJECTION: I don't need it.

Call your banker and ask him if his bank would continue corporate credit if it knew your keyman was gone?

* * * * * *

(In selling anybody)

OBJECTION: I'm medically O.K.

You look good on the outside, but you know—there's a price tag on success. Yes, you get examined every year. Your doctor looks you over, tells you you're in wonderful shape *today!* But we don't just look at today. Because we know —once we get on the risk, there's only one way we get off—when we pay your claim.

You know, Mother Nature has a way of making us a little bit older as the years go by, and gradually, we begin to fall apart. Quite often, we waited too long. Suppose we find out *if* you can still qualify!

Part V

The Success Formula: Making the Method Work

OBSTACLES TO SUCCESS AND HOW TO OVERCOME THEM

22

'You can't win 'em all'

Like all salesmen, Ben has run collision courses with a wide variety of obstacles to success. Some he's learned how to overcome. Others, he confesses, have him beat. "You can't win 'em all," he admits, "and you shouldn't expect to." Some of the obstacles Ben encounters are those any life insurance salesman might meet. Others are obstacles built in to his own method of success.

Let's look at one of those built-in obstacles, and how Ben has learned to handle it. For a complete picture of this situation, let's go back to the "closing interview." Ben, you'll recall, doesn't "close" at all, in the usual sense that he completes a sale.

The Success Formula: Making the Method Work

He can't complete a sale, because he feels he has nothing to sell. He only has something to sell *if* the man is insurable. And Ben knows the medical examination for his potential million-dollar prospect is going to be tough.

"We're going to throw the book at you," Ben warns him. "When we put up that much money, we want to make sure you look as good on the inside as you do on the outside."

Yet the medical examination is only one criterion of insurability. Home Office underwriters must assess the prospect's financial ability to continue paying premiums, his reputation, his habits, everything that bears upon him as a risk for his age. This total appraisal of the prospect's insurability is an obstacle to the sale over which Ben has no influence. Yet, the Feldman Method itself creates another obstacle at this point which Ben *can* usually handle.

Ben not only requests enough insurance from the Company to cover his client's present needs, but looks ahead, five, ten, even twenty years, and tries to anticipate his client's needs in the *future*. Most life insurance coverage solves immediate problems, but Ben seeks to provide "an option on the insurance my client will need tomorrow to solve his problems—*then*."

Because he knows his clients so well, Ben can estimate their futures, in relation to insurance needs, with a high degree of accuracy. He knows his clients' businesses should expand. And he knows, too, that the days ahead hold threats to those businesses: from inflation, from death costs to be paid in cash when most assets of the business may be tied up in inventory, machinery and land. It is the forecasting of these future needs that has consistently upped Ben's dollar volume. "By creating bigger problems in the future, my clients force me to write bigger cases."

Obstacles to Success and How to Overcome Them

He writes those "future cases" *now*. A man needs options on the additional insurance required in the years ahead, Ben realizes. But a man's health changes, and these options have to be obtained while he can still get them, while he's still insurable—and that's *now*. Ben sells today for tomorrow's needs.

But this idea of "selling ahead," so basic to Feldman's success, brings him smack up against a formidable obstacle: the traditional philosophy that life insurance underwriting may cover only the risks—only the demonstrable needs—of today. Underwriting tomorrow's needs is likely to be regarded as "speculation." Rarely does Ben fail to obtain enough coverage to solve his clients' needs for today, but Ben often has difficulty in securing underwriting approval of the sums he conjectures his clients will need for today *and* for tomorrow!

So, Ben now has another selling job ahead of him—the Company.

Every week finds Ben arguing the case of a prospect where the volume of insurance sought seems well above that allowed under traditional underwriting standards. Ben's approach is factual and hard-headed. Here's where his client's company stands today, he'll say, and here's its growth pattern. It's just a matter of projection. Here's what the balance sheet will look like ten or twenty years in the future. Here are the problems the client will have to meet then. Here's how life insurance—and only life insurance—can solve those problems. But, Ben insists to the underwriters, my client must secure his options on tomorrow today. Or he won't be able to have them at all.

So persuasive has Ben been in selling individual cases that the concept of "selling ahead" has made deep inroads into conventional underwriting practice. Today's Home Office under-

THE SUCCESS FORMULA: MAKING THE METHOD WORK

writers have gone a long way toward recognizing that they can often grant options in the insurance offered to cover tomorrow. By bringing about this radical alteration of viewpoint, Ben has, in the opinion of many experts, almost single-handedly revolutionized the underwriting of the so-called "jumbo" case. The $1,000,000 case today has become almost as commonplace as the $100,000 case was ten years ago.

Ben's big "selling ahead" cases have not turned out to be, as the underwriters feared, "speculative." The traditionally anticipated excess mortality and early claims just never materialized. In all of Ben's 27 years with the Company, he has had less than 1% of his business—less than $1,600,000—mature as death claims. Considering an exposure of some $300,000,000 of business, these losses have been dramatically below even the most optimistic underwriter's estimate.

"It's enough to shake an actuary's traditional belief in the time-honored theory of 'selection against the Company,'" says Ben. "But I have an explanation that seems to satisfy them. It's this—

"Are my clients the kind of people who are selecting against the company? Let's analyze them. They resist me. They fight me off. They use every ruse to avoid facing the facts in the picture I have painted for them as they are today—and as they will be tomorrow. Most of them don't really believe they need that amount of life insurance—now or ever. Persuading them to take the amount of insurance they will need is a tough job. There are times I almost have to 'cram' it down their throats—figuratively speaking. Of course, they thank me later—but they hate me a little when they are digging up that first premium. *No, these people aren't selecting against the Company. They're healthy and they think they are going to live forever.*

Obstacles to Success and How to Overcome Them

"Their insurance to them is money—big chunks of money—for future delivery when their families and businesses will need it most. And they pay for that protection the way they pay for everything else—even borrowing if their cash is out working elsewhere."

To sum up: Basic to Ben's success method is the concept of "selling ahead," because it unlocks the door to "jumbo" cases. But this concept carries a built-in obstacle: the opposition of traditional underwriters, particularly those who regard "selling ahead" as a license to clients to select against the Company. Ben overcomes this obstacle by his choice of clients (men who are not motivated by over-insurance—by speculation) and by his reasoned and factual presentation of individual situations.

*   *   *   *   *   *

Lapses are obstacles to insurance-selling success at any dollar-level of achievement, but big sales can occasionally mean big lapses. This is another obstacle that Ben Feldman encounters. Here's how he overcomes it—

"I have lapses," he admits, "but not in the usual sense. Actually, mine are a partial erosion in the initial amount of coverage. For example, I may have ordered a million of insurance. My prospect hasn't made up his mind how much to take—how much he thinks he needs—how much he can afford. It may take him 30 to 60 days—or even longer—to decide. My Company's maximum time limits for acceptance of the insurance without new medical evidence of insurability may be running out. So I persuade my prospect to give me his check for a month's premium (60-day option) usually on a term plan—*and for the whole million.* Within this time, he'll decide how much. Perhaps, he will buy $700,000 Whole Life. A solid sale in any man's league—but a 30% *erosion,* nevertheless, from that million of insurance originally put on the books a month before. So—it goes as a $300,000 lapse!

"No one has been hurt—there are virtually no extra issue costs—but the Company has to count it as a 30% lapse, regardless. And when one pays for $30- or $40- or $50,000,000 of business annually, it's not impossible to get $5,000,000 or more of this 'lapse erosion.' "

Even half a million dollars annually in lapses would not ordinarily commend a salesman to his Company. But "lapse erosion" is an inherent part of Ben's selling methods: it's one more way of bringing in the "jumbo" cases. So lapses of this type don't really hurt Ben; they actually seem to help him. He's the exception to the rule. "No wonder," comments Ben, "that they say they can't make regulations that will cover me or my method of operation."

But changes in needs and business requirements often threaten reduction in coverage at *any* time in the life of a policy, particularly when the policy is in six or seven figures. How does Ben handle these conventional lapse threats?

"Those first few months the big policy is in force are really critical," Ben observes. Feldman must be readily available to service his clients. With well over a quarter of a billion of life insurance on the books, that isn't always easy.

"The telephones in my office start ringing at 8 A.M.," explains Ben, "and they don't stop until ten hours later. My biggest worry is shaking myself loose early enough each day to call on new prospects—to develop new sales. But so many of my

Obstacles to Success and How to Overcome Them

policy owners—especially those with new policies—insist on dealing only with me." He *does* shake himself loose—by organization, by hiring people to do things for him, and by working seven days a week if necessary. Ben's highly personal touch helps keep down lapses in those early critical months.

"My lapse ratio after those first few months runs less than 2%," Ben reports. "Actually, once a case gets 'cemented in' in its first year, it rarely ever lapses."

Lapsing is also deterred by prepayments. "Many of my policy owners are prepaying premiums as much as twenty-five years in advance. Currently these advance premiums total in excess of a million dollars."

* * * * * *

"Lapse erosion" and "the opposition of underwriters to 'selling ahead'" are obstacles built in to the Feldman Method. Other obstacles to success are those any life-insurance salesman might encounter in the field. Here is a sampling.

"I delivered a policy for $150,000, collected the premium. About thirty days later, I received a phone call from the insured. He told me: he didn't want the policy . . . he didn't need that much insurance . . . he couldn't afford to pay the premium . . . and he threw in all the other rationale a man gives for changing his mind. He was very persuasive. He changed *my* mind about his needs. The final result was that we cut the policy in half, paid *two* annual premiums on a $75,000 policy.

"Believe it or not, within 60 days while playing cards at a friend's home, he became ill and died within a couple of days.

The Success Formula: Making the Method Work

"We had traded . . . we paid $75,000 and refunded that second premium . . . and yet we had originally stood ready to pay $150,000!"

Why did Ben fail? "I found a man who at that moment was a better salesman than I was!" Ben concedes, "That's one obstacle I've never been able to overcome."

Another selling obstacle that Ben runs into frequently is a man's pride in his own health. Ben tells this case history as an illustration:

"There was this motor freight company built around the efforts of one man. He started with $500, and, through hard work, pyramided it into a $5,000,000 company. He recognized the need for life insurance, but never had any money—at least, he never had any extra money.

"At our first meeting, he said, O.K., write me a $10,000 policy every thirty days. I told him this wouldn't work because it would require constant re-examination. The net result was that he agreed to consider $50,000. He was examined, and I asked my Company to issue the $50,000—*together with* an additional policy for $1,000,000. The man's needs were for much more than $50,000. He ran a one-man company and it needed a cushion if it should lose him—something to put a floor beneath a credit line.

"Two policies were issued. But they were highly rated for medical reasons. When I tried to place them, my client almost tossed me out. It wasn't that there was such a tremendous difference in premiums, but he simply wouldn't accept the fact that his health was below par! Nevertheless, he felt an obligation to me since I had spent time working on his problem. He finally accepted the $50,000. But what a difference—$50,000 and $1,000,000!

"I didn't give up too easily on placing the $1,000,000 policy. Months later he did agree to reconsider. Of course, now this meant re-examination. He was a busy man ... it was difficult to schedule him in for another medical. I finally did so, but the fates are strange! The doctor died before he could complete the examination. A few weeks later ... the insured died sitting in a chair in a motel in another city where he had gone on business. *A doctor died—the man died—and a year later the company died.*"

Ben admits that he loses some cases this way. "These men have pride, and their pride simply won't let them admit that the rate-up *is* reasonable because their health *has* deteriorated."

Other men defeat Ben through stubbornness. "Take the case of this young president of a closely-held corporation. He was so much a keyman that all operations were built around him. He was a money man. He was top man in sales. He was an all-around man capable of making things happen. I wrote a keyman policy in the amount of $200,000. It was a term policy with a premium of only $100 per month.

"But he was mighty stubborn about facing facts. He simply refused to talk about it. In this case, try as I might, I simply couldn't deliver that policy."

Stubbornness, pride, a client's super-salesmanship are some of the obstacles that often defeat Ben. Are there others?

"Yes," says Ben. "Some men feel they have all the life insurance they will ever need. Some insist on shopping for a bargain—and wind up buying nothing. Some seem to know more about life insurance than I do—and I have trouble. Some prefer mutual funds—special investments. There are still a few today—strange to relate—who still either don't believe in life insurance or attack it as a racket.

The Success Formula: Making the Method Work

"One way or another, I often fail to get the job done. A lot of big ones get away—and I lose potential millions in volume. Nobody else gets that business. It's just that the business isn't bought. Or, perhaps, it's just that I'm not good enough to sell it."

Ben *has* overcome most of these obstacles—often by sheer perseverance, often by restating his presentation in a variety of ways ("When they close one door, I come in by another..."). But too often, by his own high standards he feels he has failed. How does he try to improve his performance?

"In some cases," says Ben, "I don't try. I just don't waste time on the non-believers and the reformers. And when a prospect's personality and mine don't mesh, I know we'll never agree. The day is too short to throw it away on the impossible cases. You also have to know when *not* to sell!

"But the other sales that got away worry me. I know they represent big problems for somebody in the future, and I didn't get them solved. So I keep trying to find ways to sell these people."

How?

"By trying to persuade them to recognize their problems. That makes them *want* to be helped. And life insurance *can* help them. If I can only find some way—some sure-fire way—to make them recognize their problems..."

Ben Feldman knows he can't win 'em all. But he also knows he should win more of 'em. So he keeps on trying!

GUIDELINES TO SUCCESS AND HOW TO APPLY THEM | 23

'There's no limit to what a salesman can earn'

A young Australian life insurance salesman said to Feldman, "Ben, you say everything has a price. I'd like to be as successful as you. What's the price?"

"Well, for one thing my week has seven days," answered Ben. "For me," said the young man, "that's too high a price."

Success the Feldman way is only for those willing to work hard, to discipline themselves, to sacrifice present leisures for future gains.

If you are one of those people, Ben has given you a track to run on. It's a wide open track without a STOP sign. There's

The Success Formula: Making the Method Work

no limit to how far you can go. But it's no easy track. It requires all the endurance and grit and patience of the long-distance runner. Feldman didn't "make it" overnight.

"If people knew how hard I work to achieve my mastery," says Ben quoting the great Michelangelo, "it wouldn't seem so wonderful after all." It's a hard, grueling road without a single short-cut. Here you'll find no formula for instant success, no gimmicks, no magic sales talks. It's a track paved with intense effort by Ben Feldman, and it takes "guts" to run on it—day after day.

Your "track to run on" is the Feldman Method. That Method, as you already know, is in essence extremely simple. Let Ben sum it up: "All men have money problems, but *big* men have *big* money problems. Many of these problems can be solved by life insurance. Your job is to find those problems. Once you have found them, you must offer the solution in packages so simple and so concise that every word will be understood."

But a "success method," no matter how simple, is very much like a golf pro's "technique for lowering your score." Learning it is no guarantee that you'll break 100. Add hard work, and your chances improve. But you're still not necessarily in the championship class. You need something else. You need that special something that champions have. In selling, Ben Feldman has it. What is this special something?

Edwin P. Hoyt, in a book on America's top twelve salesmen (which included Ben Feldman, of course), concluded that all of these super-salesmen exhibited the same characteristics. He writes that these men are, in addition to efficient *hard workers, self-confident and self-disciplined;* they have *perseverance, flexibility, goals other than money, respect for the buyer's good*

218

GUIDELINES TO SUCCESS AND HOW TO APPLY THEM

sense, willingness to learn from others, ability to make big money; they are *perfectionists."*

Can you acquire all of these 10 success-characteristics? Certainly, Ben Feldman wasn't born with them. He acquired them. When he started selling, he had less apparent natural talent than any agent in the state. He had few friends, no influence. By his own admission, he was a "country hick," with little of the graces needed for insurance salesmanship. He had a slight impediment in his speech. He flunked the sales aptitude tests. He *had* to acquire his success-characteristics. How did he do it?

After more than a quarter of a century working with Ben, I can't be sure. But it may very well be that these success-characteristics grew out of his work *habits*—patterns of action which he repeated over and over again until they became as natural to him as breathing. These work habits can be regarded as Ben's guidelines to success. Here's a description of these habits, and how their application may have brought Ben the success-characteristics without which he never could have adventured so far into his own possibilities.

GUIDELINE TO SUCCESS #1

Form the habit of careful preparation.

Ben does this on two levels. *In general,* he keeps abreast of all relevant literature, attends sales meetings and seminars, "shop talks" with his colleagues. *In particular,* he learns everything he can about his prospect, and comes up with just the right solution to his prospect's problem, and just the right way to present it—*before* he ever goes out on that first interview.

Applying the guideline of preparation enables Ben to make a sales call with *confidence.* It's hard to believe, but there

THE SUCCESS FORMULA: MAKING THE METHOD WORK

was once a time when Ben was afraid to make a call. That time will never come again because preparation gives him a sense of certainty that dispels all doubts, nervousness and fear.

The habit of preparation is a key to acquiring the success-characteristic of self-confidence.

GUIDELINE TO SUCCESS #2

Form the habit of organizing your work and each work day.

Here's how Ben Feldman organizes—

First, he lists *what* has to be done in order of its importance—"first things come first."

Next, he decides *when* they should be done. He thinks ahead. He plans his sales calls, his service calls, his office work for a whole week. Then he breaks that down into days. Then he breaks his days down into hours. Planning a whole week may seem like a difficult task, but planning it hour by hour becomes, as Ben puts it, "do-able." Ben organizes his time to get the most out of every minute.

Then, knowing *what* he has to do, and *when* he has to do it, he decides on *how* to do it best. Like every step in Ben's program of organization, this final step is worked out in meticulous detail.

Applying the guideline of organization forces Ben "to do what he knows he should do, and avoid doing what he knows he shouldn't do." That, you recall, is Ben's definition of *self-discipline.*

The habit of organization is a key to acquiring the success-characteristic of self-discipline.

GUIDELINES TO SUCCESS AND HOW TO APPLY THEM

GUIDELINE TO SUCCESS #3

Form the habit of creative hard work.

Ben works on his ideas, then reworks them over and over again, until his presentations are exactly the way he wants them —simply flawless and flawlessly simple. Similarly, when a prospect says, "No," Ben will rework his approach over and over again to achieve that ultimate "Yes."

Applying the guideline of reworking his material equips Ben with a practical formula for "staying with" an idea that refuses to jell, or a client who refuses to be sold. He knows that with this formula, his *perseverance* has a good chance of paying off.

The habit of reworking your material is a key to acquiring the success-characteristic of perseverance.

GUIDELINE TO SUCCESS #4

Form the habit of fitting individual needs.

Ben never sells just policies. He sells "tailored dollars" —packages of money fitted to the *specific* financial needs of his prospect.

Applying the guideline of filling individual needs prevents Ben's thinking from falling into a mould. Each man's needs differ. Ben must come up with different packages. Ben can *not* provide *different* packages with a rigid approach. He must be flexible.

The habit of filling individual needs is a key to acquiring the success-characteristic of flexibility.

221

The Success Formula: Making the Method Work

GUIDELINE TO SUCCESS #5

Form the habit of thinking solely in your client's best interests.

To Ben Feldman, selling insurance *is* thinking in terms of his client's interest. He understands the great good that life insurance brings to so many people, in so many different ways. It creates the dollars that underwrite a man's future, that conserve the estates older men spent all their years building up. It establishes credit, raises cash, builds business. It guarantees the education of a man's children, pays the mortgage on his home, provides for his old age. It throws a shield of financial protection around his widow. It gives a man an option on tomorrow.

Ben doesn't make sales. He makes "dreams come true."

Applying the guideline of thinking in terms of the client's interest gives Ben aspirations that transcend business transactions, *goals other than money*. He has a deep desire to be of help, to eliminate the security- and happiness-gaps in his clients' lives. He feels a single-minded zeal to bring the benefits of life insurance to as many people as possible.

The habit of thinking in terms of your client's interest is a key to acquiring the success-characteristic of having goals other than money.

GUIDELINE TO SUCCESS #6

Form the habit of selling yourself on what you're selling.

Ben has never doubted the value of life insurance in general. But he has constantly wrestled with the problem of finding *the best possible* adaptation of life insurance to a man's particular problem. He is never satisfied until he has probed all

Guidelines to Success and How to Apply them

possibilities, analyzed his solution for all weaknesses—and eliminated them. Only when he's certain that his solution can *not* be improved, is he "sold on it" himself. Then, and only then, will he try to sell it to his client.

Applying the guideline of selling your product to yourself first shows *respect for your client's good sense.* Ben knows that the men with whom he deals are successful business men who have the good sense to see through a flawed presentation. He also knows they have the good sense to recognize a presentation that is *certain* to fill their needs. Ben's test of that certainty is his ability to *pre*-sell his package to the toughest client of them all—himself.

The habit of selling yourself on what you're selling is a key to acquiring the success-characteristic of respect for the buyer's good sense.

GUIDELINE TO SUCCESS #7

Form the habit of continuous study.

Ben's studies didn't end with his C.L.U. degree. Nor does it end with his great sales achievements. Although Ben long ago completed his formal education in insurance, and developed a highly successful Method of his own, he still continues to study. His reasons: Learning *more* may help him sell some of the ones that "got away." It will help him, as well, to cope with the constantly changing pattern of legislation and economics which has so much influence on his clientele and his type of life insurance sales.

By applying the habit of continual study, Ben keeps his mind open to new ideas, and demonstrates his *willingness to learn from others*. There's no mental resistance when others in his

THE SUCCESS FORMULA: MAKING THE METHOD WORK

field come up with a usable power phrase, or a new approach, or a "package" idea that works. Ben accepts this help gladly, adopts the new concepts, and makes them his own. It's a habit that constantly makes him stronger as a salesman.

The habit of continuous study is a key to acquiring the success-characteristic of willingness to learn from others.

GUIDELINE TO SUCCESS #8

Form the habit of constantly increasing your goals.

"There's no limit," claims Ben, "to what a salesman can earn." His career proves it. Every time Ben reached a dollar-goal, he set himself a higher one. Even today, at a pinnacle of achievement unmatched by any other salesman in his field, he keeps on setting higher and higher goals for himself. He'll never stop.

Applying the habit of constantly increasing his goals spurs Ben on to constantly increasing his earnings. The key word here is "constantly." Men who are not big money-makers are satisfied when they reach a certain plateau of achievement. Ben is never satisfied. This accounts, in large part, for his ability to achieve larger and larger financial goals.

The habit of constantly increasing your goals is a key to acquiring the success-characteristic of being able to make big money.

GUIDELINE TO SUCCESS #9

Form the habit of seeking perfection.

To Ben, no detail is too small. He is constantly checking and rechecking every item relating to every case. And then he checks it again. Reviewing a case to Ben, doesn't simply mean, "Is it there?" It means also, "Is it *right?*" Ben will never settle for anything if there's even the slightest question about it in his mind. He'll spend hours, days sometimes, erasing all doubts. For instance, Ben's interviews are more than a series of disturbing questions—more than carefully honed power phrases—more than just exactly the right combination of logic and emotion. He will work two months, if necessary, on one presentation until it is right.

By getting into the habit of checking and double-checking every detail of his work, Ben not only avoids errors, but creates better products and better presentations. No man is perfect, but Ben aims for perfection—which is the definition of a *perfectionist.* "If you aim for perfection and fall short of your aim," says Ben, "you won't fall too far from the top." *The habit of checking and double-checking is a key to acquiring the success-characteristic of becoming a perfectionist.*

And this perfection shows up in many different ways. For example, Ben was impressed early with the fact that *how* you say something may be even more important than *what* you say. So some of Ben's success must hinge on how he uses his carefully fashioned phrases—the rhythms of speech, his gestures and his facial expressions. They all work for Ben because he has tied them to his own personality with perfection.

* * * * * *

The success-characteristics possessed by America's leading salesmen may, therefore, be acquired basically through good work habits. But, put all the nine success-characteristics I've outlined together, and they still won't result in great success without that added ingredient *efficient hard work.* Can the ability to work hard, as Ben works hard, twelve hours a day, even seven days a week if necessary, week after week, at record-breaking pitch, be acquired?

The Success Formula: Making the Method Work

If you have a burning desire to win, a dissatisfaction that keeps driving you on, an insatiable passion for success, to be the best, you *will* work hard. But there's a danger. You may work *too* hard. You may be setting a schedule for yourself that no man could sustain on a regular basis. Your failure to do so might frustrate you, shatter your confidence, severely hurt your chances of success as a salesman. So . . .

GUIDELINE TO SUCCESS #10

Form the habit of setting achievable deadlines.

Feldman does just that. His three applications a week *are* achievable. Whenever he sets himself a task—whether it's digesting a new policy or setting up a quota—he breaks it down into small segments that he can handle. He knows that if he tried to eat a two-pound steak at one gulp, he'd go hungry. He eats a bite at a time.

By applying the habit of setting achievable deadlines, Ben works efficiently. That means, he works only as hard as he has to work. There is no energy wasted on impossible-to-achieve goals. He never works too hard. Hard work doesn't seem like hard work when every minute is productive.

The habit of setting achievable deadlines is the key to efficient hard work.

* * * * * *

You now know the Feldman Method. You now have an idea of how Ben acquired the success-characteristics for making that Method work. Can *you* combine these success-characteristics with the Feldman Method to achieve the same success as Ben Feldman?

Guidelines to Success and How to Apply them

It would be patently absurd to answer with an unqualified, "Yes." The individual complexity of each human being makes it impossible to apply any sweeping generalization. But one thing is certain: Ben is a rarity, a genius in the field of selling who may not be equalled for another century. The chances are against your becoming another Ben Feldman. But—

But if success is important to you—if the Feldman Method, with its uncompromising emphasis on conviction, hard work, perfection, increasingly difficult goals, persistence and self-organization is *acceptable* to you—you can benefit by the lesson of Ben's career. It will help you realize your potential. It will help you increase your income. It will help you serve your community better.

Ben Feldman is a dedicated and sincere man. A quietly confident man. A man who's humble, soft-voiced, interested in the person he's talking with, involved. He's a man who speaks slowly and surely. He's a gentle man who never pushes. He's your friend. He's your neighbor. He's a shoulder to lean on. He's a helping hand. He's the guy who's always there when you need him. He's the man whose low-keyed soft-sell approach is the key to fortunes. It unlocks the hearts and minds of men . . . so he can serve them.

He is a great salesman. But he wasn't born to this greatness, nor did he have it thrust on him. He made himself great. Not through arrogance, power or brutality, but through quiet devotion to a mission—bringing the answers of life insurance to as many people as possible. He's that good guy who does finish first—an ordinary man who's scaled extraordinary sales heights no one even dreamed of before.

Recommended Readings

- Think and Grow Rich by Napoleon Hill

- The Master-Key to Riches by Napoleon Hill

- The Law of Success In Sixteen Lessons (2 Disc Set) by Napoleon Hill

- Warren Buffett Talks to MBA Students by Warren Buffett

- How I Learned the Secrets of Success in Selling by Frank Bettger

- You Can Still Make It In The Market by Nicolas Darvas

- The Richest Man in Babylon - Illustrated by George S. Clason

- Invest like a Billionaire: If you are not watching the best investor in the world, who are you watching?

- Show Me Your Options! The Guide to Complete Confidence for Every Stock and Options Trader Seeking Consistent, Predictable Returns
By Steve Burns, Christopher Ebert

- Back to School: Question & Answer Session with Business Students by Warren Buffett

- New Trader, Rich Trader: How to Make Money in the Stock Market by Steve Burns

Available at   www.bnpublishing.com